How To Stop Being A Narcissist, Compulsive Liar, Abusive Partner, and A Toxic Person (4 Books in 1)

Guide to Build Long Lasting Healthy Relationships

Dennis Lee

Contents

Book 1

How To Stop Being A Narcissist

Introduction

In today's fast-paced and increasingly interconnected world, the quality of our relationships plays a significant role in determining our happiness, mental well-being, and overall success. As we interact with family, friends, coworkers, and romantic partners, fostering positive connections built on trust, respect, and genuine care for one another is essential. Unfortunately, some individuals may exhibit behaviors that harm these relationships, leading to a cycle of negativity, disappointment, and failed connections.

This book is designed to help individuals recognize and address the traits holding them back from nurturing healthy relationships. By integrating four distinct books into one comprehensive guide, this book aims to thoroughly understand the interconnected nature of narcissism, compulsive lying, abusive behavior, and toxic personality traits. It offers practical guidance and evidence-based strategies to help individuals break free from these patterns, cultivate self-awareness, and ultimately improve the quality of their relationships.

The journey toward self-improvement is not easy, and it requires a deep level of self-awareness, commitment, and willingness to change. Furthermore, it is essential to acknowledge that change is a gradual process and that overcoming these negative behaviors will not happen overnight. This book will be your ally throughout this process, offering actionable advice, reflective exercises, and real-life examples to help you navigate the challenges and successes of personal growth.

In the 1st book, we will explore the concept of narcissism, its root causes, and its impact on one's relationships. Then, we will provide the following:

- Practical advice on challenging selfish thoughts and behaviors.
- Developing empathy and emotional intelligence.
- Ultimately building healthy self-esteem.

The second part of the book addresses the issue of compulsive lying, delving into the psychology behind this behavior and its effects on trust and credibility. Finally, we will offer strategies to help individuals resist the urge to lie, face the truth, and rebuild trust in their relationships.

In the third book, we will focus on abusive behavior in relationships, examining various types of abuse, their underlying patterns, and their consequences on both the abuser and the victim. Finally, we will share techniques for cultivating healthy relationship skills, managing emotions, and establishing boundaries and accountability.

Lastly, the 4th book will discuss how to detoxify one's personality by identifying toxic traits and developing emotional intelligence. We will provide the following:

- Guidance on nurturing positive relationships.
- Creating a supportive social circle.
- Celebrating personal growth and change.

Throughout the book, you will find integrated workbook sections and exercises designed to facilitate self-assessment, self-reflection, and practical application of the strategies discussed. These tools will empower you to take an active role in your journey towards self-improvement and building long-lasting healthy relationships.
By committing to this journey, you take a brave and essential step toward personal growth and genuine happiness. We hope this book will serve as a valuable resource and guide as you embark on creating and sustaining positive, fulfilling connections in your life.

Chapter 1

Understanding Narcissism

Definition and Types of Narcissism

As a personality trait, narcissism originates in Greek mythology, where Narcissus, a beautiful youth, fell in love with his own reflection and ultimately died from his self-obsession. In psychology, narcissism is characterized by an inflated sense of self-worth, a constant need for admiration, and a lack of empathy for others. It's important to acknowledge that narcissism exists on a spectrum, and everyone possesses varying degrees of narcissistic traits. These traits can be adaptive and functional to an extent, but when they become excessive, they can lead to detrimental consequences in interpersonal relationships.

Two primary subtypes of narcissism are recognized: grandiose and vulnerable. Grandiose narcissism, commonly known as overt narcissism, is typified by an exaggerated sense of superiority, entitlement, and a tendency to exploit and manipulate others for personal gain. Individuals with grandiose narcissism often display extroverted, assertive, and self-confident behavior. In contrast, vulnerable narcissism, sometimes called covert narcissism, manifests as a deep-seated sense of inadequacy, extreme sensitivity to criticism, and a propensity to harbor resentment and envy. Although both subtypes can damage relationships, they present differently and necessitate tailored approaches for personal growth and change.

Root Causes of Narcissism

The development of narcissistic traits can be attributed to a complex interplay of genetic, psychological, and environmental factors. Therefore, no single factor can definitively determine whether someone will develop pathological narcissism, but the combination of these influences shapes one's personality.

Childhood experiences have a significant impact on the development of narcissism. In some cases, parents' or caregivers' excessive praise, indulgence, or overvaluation can foster an inflated sense of self-worth and entitlement. Conversely, neglect, excessive criticism, or a lack of emotional support during childhood can also give rise to narcissistic traits as a defense mechanism to cope with feelings of inadequacy and insecurity.

Societal and cultural factors, such as an emphasis on individualism, success, competition, and material wealth, can contribute to developing and reinforcing narcissistic tendencies. In addition, the advent and proliferation of social media platforms and the culture of self-promotion have intensified this issue, as they often encourage and reward self-centered and self-aggrandizing behavior.

Recognizing Narcissistic Traits in Oneself

The journey towards overcoming narcissism begins with identifying and acknowledging the narcissistic traits within oneself. This can be challenging, as self-awareness and introspection do not come naturally to those with pronounced narcissistic tendencies. Some common indicators of narcissism include:

- An unrelenting need for admiration and validation
- A sense of entitlement and expectation of preferential treatment
- Exaggerating one's achievements, abilities, and talents
- Belittling, demeaning, or devaluing others to enhance one's self-image
- Exploiting others for personal benefit or advancement
- Difficulty empathizing with and understanding others' feelings and needs
- An aversion to criticism or accepting responsibility for one's actions

By recognizing these traits within yourself and confronting them honestly, you can initiate the process of self-improvement and work towards cultivating healthier, more fulfilling relationships. In the subsequent chapters, we will provide the following:

- Practical advice on challenging selfish thoughts and behaviors.
- Developing empathy and emotional intelligence.
- Fostering balanced self-esteem.

How does your understanding of narcissism affect your view of yourself and your relationships with others?

Can you identify any narcissistic traits or behaviors you may have exhibited in the past? How did they impact your life and relationships?

What steps can you take to be more self-aware and prevent narcissistic tendencies from controlling your actions?

Chapter 2

Breaking Narcissistic Patterns

Narcissism is a complex and multifaceted personality disorder that can profoundly affect those suffering from it. It is characterized by an inflated sense of self-importance, a constant need for admiration and attention, and a lack of empathy toward others. As a result, selfish individuals often struggle to maintain healthy relationships and may engage in manipulative or abusive behavior. However, breaking narcissistic patterns and building more beneficial relationships through self-awareness, empathy, humility, boundary-setting, and self-care is possible.

Developing self-awareness is a crucial first step in breaking narcissistic patterns. Narcissistic individuals may have difficulty recognizing their behavior and how it affects others. Regular self-reflection can help you understand how your thoughts, feelings, and actions contribute to selfish behavior. Keeping a journal, practicing mindfulness, or working with a therapist are all effective ways to cultivate self-awareness.

Seeking feedback from others is also an essential aspect of breaking narcissistic patterns. Narcissistic individuals may have difficulty receiving criticism, but it is integral to personal growth and development. Listening actively to others' perspectives and considering their feedback with an open mind can help you identify areas for improvement and make positive changes in your behavior. It can also be helpful to seek input from multiple sources, such as family, friends, colleagues, or mental health professionals, to understand how your behavior affects others.

Empathy is another key trait that narcissistic individuals may struggle with. Empathy involves understanding and relating to others' emotions and experiences, which is essential for building healthy relationships. Practice active listening and ask questions to understand others' perspectives. Please try to put yourself in their shoes and validate their feelings. This can help you develop stronger connections with others and build more fulfilling relationships.

Humility is also a necessary trait to cultivate when breaking narcissistic patterns. Narcissistic individuals may have an inflated sense of self-importance and struggle to admit fault or make mistakes. However, acknowledging your limitations and taking responsibility for your actions can be a decisive step toward building healthier relationships. Be open to feedback, apologize when necessary, and show a willingness to learn from your mistakes.

Setting boundaries is another crucial component of breaking narcissistic patterns. Narcissistic individuals may struggle to respect others' boundaries, leading to conflict and damaged relationships. Identify your limitations and communicate them clearly to others. Respect others' boundaries as well and avoid crossing them. This can help build trust and respect in your relationships and create healthier dynamics.

Finally, self-care is essential for breaking narcissistic patterns and building healthier relationships. Selfish individuals may focus too much on external validation and neglect their needs. Prioritize self-care by engaging in activities that bring you joy and fulfillment, such as exercise, creative pursuits, or spending time with loved ones. Seek therapy or professional support to address any underlying issues or trauma.

Breaking narcissistic patterns is an ongoing process that requires commitment, self-reflection, and a willingness to learn and grow. It may be challenging sometimes, but the rewards of healthier relationships and improved well-being are well worth the effort. Remember to be patient with yourself and celebrate your progress along the way. By developing self-awareness, empathy, humility, boundary-setting, and self-care, you can break narcissistic patterns and build healthier relationships for yourself and those around you. With time and effort, you can cultivate a deeper understanding of yourself and others and create more fulfilling relationships grounded in mutual respect, empathy, and trust.

What specific narcissistic patterns have you noticed in your behavior or thinking? How have these patterns affected your life?

How can you actively work to break these patterns and create healthier habits?

Reflect on a recent situation where you broke a narcissistic pattern. What strategies did you use and what was the outcome?

Chapter 3

Building Healthy Self-Esteem

Self-esteem is a fundamental aspect of our mental health and overall well-being. It influences how we perceive ourselves, interact with others, and navigate the world around us. A positive sense of self-worth is essential for healthy functioning in all areas of life, while low self-esteem can lead to feelings of inadequacy, shame, and self-doubt. However, it is possible to build healthy self-esteem through self-reflection, self-care, and positive self-talk.

To better understand the significance of healthy self-esteem, let's explore the story of Emily in more depth. Emily was a successful businesswoman who had worked hard to achieve her goals. Yet, despite her accomplishments, she often felt like she needed to improve. As a result, Emily would constantly compare herself to others and criticize herself for flaws or mistakes.

Emily's low self-esteem affected many aspects of her life, including her relationships. She would often seek validation from others, constantly seeking approval and reassurance from her friends, family, and coworkers. As a result, Emily struggled to trust herself, frequently relying on others to make decisions and validate her choices. As a result, Emily's relationships suffered, and she experienced feelings of isolation and loneliness.

Emily's story highlights the importance of building healthy self-esteem. When we value ourselves and our abilities, we are better equipped to navigate life's challenges, make decisions, and form positive relationships with others. Building healthy self-esteem can be challenging, but it is an essential step toward personal growth and fulfillment.

One way to build healthy self-esteem is through self-reflection. First, identify your strengths and accomplishments and areas where you need improvement. Then, please make a list and revisit it regularly to remind yourself of your value and progress. Reflecting on your past successes can help you build confidence in your abilities and recognize the value you bring to your relationships and work.

Another way to build healthy self-esteem is through self-care. Taking care of your physical and emotional needs is essential to your well-being. Consider engaging in activities that bring you joy and fulfillment, such as exercise, healthy eating, or relaxation techniques like meditation or journaling. By prioritizing self-care, you can create a positive self-love and self-worth feedback loop.

Surrounding yourself with positive people who support and encourage you is also essential to building healthy self-esteem. Seek out individuals who lift you, celebrate your achievements, and validate your feelings. Surrounding yourself with a positive support system can help you cultivate a positive self-image and reinforce your self-worth.

In addition to surrounding yourself with positive people, limiting your exposure to negativity is essential. Social media and other online platforms can be a breeding ground for negative self-talk and low self-esteem. Recognizing the negative impact of constant social media exposure on our mental health and well-being is critical. Consider taking breaks from social media and limiting your exposure to negative news or content.

Lastly, practicing positive self-talk is an essential element of building healthy self-esteem. Getting caught up in negative self-talk and beliefs that we are not good enough is easy. However, this negative self-talk can damage our self-esteem and make us feel inadequate. Instead, try to focus on your strengths and achievements and celebrate them regularly. Utilize affirmations or mantras to reinforce positive beliefs about yourself, such as "I am worthy of love and respect" or "I am capable and confident." You can cultivate a more positive and healthy self-image by practicing positive self-talk.

Building healthy self-esteem is an ongoing process that requires patience and commitment. Recognizing that progress takes time is essential, and it's okay to experience setbacks. Be kind to yourself and celebrate your progress, no matter how small. Over time, you can overcome negative self-talk and beliefs and cultivate stronger self-worth and confidence.

It's also important to recognize that building healthy self-esteem is not a one-time event but an ongoing journey. As we navigate the challenges of life, our self-esteem may fluctuate. It's important to remember that setbacks and negative experiences are a normal part of life, and they don't define us. Instead, focus on your progress and the positive steps you're taking toward building healthy self-esteem.

In addition to self-reflection, self-care, and positive self-talk, there are other strategies you can use to build healthy self-esteem. One such method is to practice self-compassion. Self-compassion involves treating yourself with kindness, understanding, and forgiveness when you face challenges or make mistakes. By practicing self-compassion, you can cultivate a more positive and accepting attitude toward yourself, increasing self-esteem and well-being.

Another strategy for building healthy self-esteem is to set achievable goals and work towards them. Setting goals that align with your values and interests can help you make sense of purpose and accomplishment. You can also build confidence in your abilities by achieving your goals and reinforcing your self-worth.

It's also important to challenge negative self-talk and beliefs. Negative self-talk can be a self-fulfilling prophecy, leading us to believe we are not good enough or capable of success. Instead, challenge these negative beliefs with evidence that supports your strengths and accomplishments. For example, if you're struggling with imposter syndrome, remind yourself of your achievements and your skills and knowledge.

Building healthy self-esteem is essential for personal growth and well-being and plays a significant role in our relationships with others. When we have healthy self-esteem, we are more likely to form positive relationships with others, set boundaries, and advocate for our needs and desires. On the other hand, when we struggle with low self-esteem, we may have difficulty forming and maintaining healthy relationships.

If you're struggling with low self-esteem, seek support from a mental health professional. A therapist can help you work through underlying issues contributing to your low self-esteem and provide strategies for building healthy self-esteem.

Building healthy self-esteem is a critical step toward personal growth and well-being. You can cultivate a more positive and healthy self-image by engaging in self-reflection, self-care, positive self-talk, and other strategies. Building healthy self-esteem is an ongoing journey, and progress takes time. Be kind to yourself, celebrate your progress, and seek support when needed. You can lead a more fulfilling and satisfying life with healthy self-esteem.

How do you currently view yourself? Do you feel that you have a healthy level of self-esteem?

What are some achievements or qualities you are proud of? How can you celebrate and acknowledge these aspects of yourself more often?

What steps can you take to improve your self-esteem and foster a more positive self-image?

Chapter 4

Narcissism & Relationships

Narcissism is a personality trait characterized by grandiosity, a need for admiration, and a lack of empathy for others. While some level of narcissism is normal and healthy, excessive narcissism can be detrimental to relationships. In this chapter, we will explore the impact of narcissism on relationships and provide strategies for managing narcissistic tendencies and building healthy relationships.

Narcissistic individuals often prioritize their own needs and desires over those of others. They may struggle to empathize with others, take criticism or feedback, and prioritize the well-being of their partners. Narcissistic tendencies can lead to negative relationship behaviors, including emotional manipulation, gaslighting, and verbal or physical abuse.

For individuals in relationships with narcissists, it can be challenging to navigate these behaviors and maintain a healthy relationship. However, managing narcissistic tendencies and building healthy relationships with open communication, empathy, and boundary-setting is possible.

Open communication is one of the critical strategies for managing narcissistic tendencies in relationships. Individuals with narcissistic tendencies may struggle with communication and expressing emotions, leading to misunderstandings and conflict. However, you can build trust and mutual understanding by prioritizing open communication and active listening to your partner.

Empathy is another critical element in managing narcissistic tendencies in relationships. Selfish individuals may struggle with empathy, but it is possible to develop this skill through active listening and trying to understand your partner's perspective. By demonstrating empathy, you can create a more supportive and nurturing relationship that prioritizes the needs and desires of both partners.

Another critical strategy for managing narcissistic tendencies in relationships is setting healthy boundaries. Individuals with narcissistic tendencies may struggle to respect the boundaries of others, which can lead to resentment, frustration, and exhaustion. However, setting clear and consistent boundaries and communicating them openly with your partner can create a more respectful and supportive relationship. Recognizing the signs of emotional manipulation and abuse in relationships is also essential. Narcissistic individuals may use dynamic manipulation tactics such as gaslighting or stonewalling to control their partners and maintain power in the relationship. It is crucial to recognize these behaviors and seek support from a mental health professional or domestic violence advocate if necessary.

If you are in a relationship with a narcissistic individual, it is essential to recognize that change is

possible but requires effort and commitment from both partners. In addition, selfish individuals may struggle with self-reflection and accountability, so seeking support from a mental health professional specializing in narcissistic personality disorder may be helpful.
In addition to seeking professional support, there are other strategies that both partners can use to build a healthier relationship. These include:

- Practicing active listening and empathy
- Fostering open and honest communication
- Respecting each other's boundaries and needs
- Prioritizing self-care and personal growth
- Celebrating each other's accomplishments and strengths

Building a healthy relationship with a narcissistic individual is difficult, but it is possible with the proper support and strategies. It is essential to prioritize your well-being and safety in any relationship and seek help if necessary.

Sometimes, it may be necessary to end the relationship if the narcissistic individual is unwilling or unable to change their behavior. Ending a relationship can be challenging, but it is essential to prioritize your safety and well-being above all else.
It's important to note that not all individuals with narcissistic tendencies are diagnosed with narcissistic personality disorder (NPD). NPD is a diagnosable mental health condition, and individuals with this disorder may require specialized treatment from a mental health professional.

However, it's also important to recognize that even individuals who do not meet the diagnostic criteria for NPD can exhibit narcissistic tendencies that can negatively impact their relationships. Therefore, it's essential to focus on the behaviors and their impact on the relationship rather than trying to diagnose the individual with a specific disorder.

One of the challenges of being in a relationship with a narcissistic individual is the emotional toll it can take on the partner. Selfish individuals may have a heightened need for admiration and use their partners to fulfill it. Unfortunately, this can lead to the partner feeling like they are constantly walking on eggshells or feeling like they are not enough.

In addition to managing the impact of narcissistic tendencies on the relationship, partners of selfish individuals need to prioritize their self-care and well-being. This may include seeking support from a therapist, setting healthy boundaries, and engaging in activities that promote emotional and physical health. For individuals who recognize narcissistic tendencies in themselves, taking steps toward managing these tendencies in relationships is essential. This may include seeking support from a mental health professional and practicing self-reflection, empathy, and self-care.

It's also essential to recognize that building healthy relationships takes effort and commitment from both partners. It's vital to prioritize open communication, mutual respect, and empathy in any relationship, regardless of whether one or both partners exhibit narcissistic tendencies.

In summary, narcissism can significantly impact relationships, but it is possible to manage narcissistic tendencies and build healthy relationships with open communication, empathy, and boundary-setting. Recognizing the signs of emotional manipulation and abuse is crucial, and seeking support from a mental health professional or domestic violence advocate may be necessary in some cases. Building a healthy relationship with a narcissistic individual requires prioritizing your well-being and safety, seeking support when necessary, and committing to open communication, mutual respect, and empathy.

How has narcissism impacted your past and current
relationships? Can you identify specific instances where
it may have played a role?

What steps can you take to ensure narcissism does not
negatively affect your relationships in the future?

How can you work on improving your empathy and
understanding towards others to build healthier
relationships?

Chapter 5

Addressing Vulnerability & Shame

Vulnerability and shame are two emotions that can significantly impact our lives and relationships. While vulnerability is often associated with openness and connection, shame can hinder meaningful connections and personal growth. In this chapter, we will explore the impact of vulnerability and shame on our lives and provide strategies for addressing these emotions and building more meaningful and fulfilling relationships.

Vulnerability is the willingness to open up and expose our true selves to others. It requires us to let go of our defenses and be honest about our feelings, thoughts, and experiences. Vulnerability can be difficult, as it requires us to face our fears of rejection and criticism.

However, vulnerability can also be incredibly rewarding. When we are vulnerable with others, we create opportunities for deeper connections and intimacy. By sharing our struggles and challenges, we invite others to share their experiences and offer support and empathy.

On the other hand, shame is a feeling of deep embarrassment and self-consciousness. Various experiences, including past trauma, social comparison, and negative self-talk, can trigger shame. Shame can be a barrier to vulnerability and connection, creating a sense of unworthiness and inadequacy.

Addressing vulnerability and shame requires self-awareness and a willingness to explore these emotions. It can be challenging to confront these emotions, but doing so can lead to personal growth and deeper connections with others.

One strategy for addressing vulnerability and shame is to practice self-compassion. Self-compassion involves treating ourselves with kindness and understanding, even in complex emotions. By practicing self-compassion, we can create a sense of safety and security within ourselves, which can help us to be more vulnerable and open with others.

Another essential strategy is to identify and challenge negative self-talk. Shame is often fueled by negative self-talk and self-criticism. Identifying these thoughts and questioning their validity can shift our perspective and cultivate a more positive and compassionate inner dialogue.

Cultivating a supportive network of friends, family, and professionals who can provide empathy and support is also essential. When we have a support system, we feel less alone and more capable of facing our vulnerabilities and addressing our shame.

One common barrier to vulnerability is fear of rejection or criticism. It's essential to recognize that rejection and criticism are a normal part of life and relationships. By reframing rejection and criticism as opportunities for growth and learning, we can become more resilient and less fearful of vulnerability.

It's also essential to recognize that vulnerability is a two-way street. When we are vulnerable with others, we create opportunities for them to be vulnerable with us. This reciprocity can lead to deeper connections and greater intimacy in relationships.

In some cases, addressing vulnerability and shame may require the support of a mental health professional. A therapist can provide guidance and support as you navigate these challenging emotions and help you develop strategies for building more meaningful and fulfilling relationships.

Another aspect of addressing vulnerability and shame is acknowledging and accepting imperfections. It's important to remember that no one is perfect, and we all have flaws and make mistakes. However, these imperfections can help us be more compassionate towards ourselves and others and create an environment where vulnerability is valued.

In addition, practicing mindfulness can be a powerful tool for addressing vulnerability and shame.

Mindfulness involves paying attention to the present moment with curiosity and non-judgment. By practicing mindfulness, we can become more aware of our emotions and thoughts and learn to respond to them more compassionately and understanding.

Finally, it's essential to recognize that vulnerability and shame are complex emotions that may require ongoing attention and effort. Building a practice of vulnerability and self-compassion takes time and patience and may involve setbacks and challenges. It's important to be gentle with ourselves and to celebrate our progress, no matter how small.

One powerful way to address vulnerability and shame in relationships is to create a culture of openness. This involves intentionally creating an environment where exposure is valued and encouraged. This can include setting aside time for meaningful conversations, being open and honest about our emotions and experiences, and expressing gratitude and appreciation for each other.

Another critical aspect of building healthy relationships is setting and respecting boundaries. Boundaries are essential to maintaining a sense of safety and security in relationships. They help us to communicate our needs and expectations and create a space where vulnerability and intimacy can thrive.

Addressing vulnerability and shame requires a commitment to self-growth and a willingness to be vulnerable with ourselves and others. By cultivating self-compassion, challenging negative self-talk, building a supportive network, reframing rejection and criticism, acknowledging imperfections, practicing mindfulness, and creating a culture of vulnerability, we can begin to make more meaningful and fulfilling relationships.

In conclusion, vulnerability and shame can be challenging emotions to address, but they are essential for building healthy and fulfilling relationships. By cultivating self-compassion, challenging negative self-talk, building a supportive network, and creating a culture of vulnerability, we can break down barriers to meaningful connections and personal growth. If exposure and shame are overwhelming, seeking support from a mental health professional may be helpful. Remember that vulnerability is a sign of strength, and by embracing it, we can create a more fulfilling and meaningful life.

How comfortable are you with expressing vulnerability? What challenges do you face when trying to be open about your emotions?

Can you identify any instances where shame has influenced your actions or decisions? How did it impact the outcome?

What strategies can you implement to confront and overcome feelings of vulnerability and shame?

Chapter 6

Managing Narcissistic Tendencies in Social Situations

Managing narcissistic tendencies in social settings can be challenging, but it is essential for building healthy relationships and navigating social situations with grace and empathy. This chapter will explore strategies for managing narcissistic tendencies in social settings and creating more meaningful and fulfilling relationships. Narcissistic tendencies can manifest in a variety of ways in social settings. For example, selfish individuals may dominate conversations, seek attention and admiration, and have difficulty empathizing with others. They may also have a heightened sense of entitlement and a tendency to belittle or dismiss the perspectives and experiences of others.

Building empathy and understanding is one key strategy for managing narcissistic tendencies in social settings. This involves:

- Actively listening to others.
- Acknowledging their perspectives and experiences.

- Responding with compassion and respect. Another essential strategy is recognizing and challenging the impulse to dominate conversations and seek attention. Narcissistic individuals may need to be the center of attention in social situations, but this can create a sense of discomfort and disconnection with others. By actively listening to others and allowing them to share their perspectives and experiences, we create opportunities for deeper connections and understanding. In addition to building empathy and understanding, setting healthy boundaries in social settings is essential. Edges help us to communicate our needs and expectations and create a sense of safety and security in social situations. This may include limiting the time spent in social settings or establishing guidelines for communication and behavior.

Another critical aspect of managing narcissistic tendencies in social settings is recognizing and addressing the impact of past experiences and trauma. For example, narcissistic tendencies may be rooted in past experiences of rejection, abandonment, or emotional pain. By addressing these underlying experiences and trauma, we can begin to heal and build healthier relationships.

In some cases, managing narcissistic tendencies in social settings may require the support of a mental health professional. A therapist can provide guidance and support as you navigate these challenging emotions and help you develop strategies for building more meaningful and fulfilling relationships.

Another strategy for managing narcissistic tendencies in social settings is to practice gratitude and humility. This involves recognizing and appreciating the contributions and experiences of others and expressing gratitude and appreciation for their presence in our lives. Practicing gratitude and humility creates a sense of connection and meaning in social settings and reduces the impulse to seek attention or dominate conversations. It's also important to recognize that managing narcissistic tendencies in social settings requires ongoing effort and attention. Likewise, building healthy relationships and navigating social situations with empathy and grace takes time and patience and may involve setbacks and challenges.

One powerful way to manage narcissistic tendencies in social settings is to engage in acts of kindness and generosity. This involves reaching out to others, offering support and empathy, and expressing gratitude and appreciation for their presence in our lives. By engaging in acts of kindness and generosity, we create opportunities for deeper connections and understanding and reduce the impulse to seek attention or dominate conversations.

Finally, it's essential to prioritize self-care and well-being in social settings. Narcissistic tendencies can be draining and exhausting, and taking breaks and engaging in activities that promote emotional and physical health is essential. This may include setting aside time for self-reflection, practicing mindfulness, or engaging in activities that bring us joy and fulfillment. In conclusion, managing narcissistic tendencies in social settings is essential for building healthy and fulfilling relationships. By building empathy and understanding, setting healthy boundaries, addressing past experiences and trauma, practicing gratitude and humility, engaging in acts of kindness and generosity, and prioritizing self-care and well-being, we can navigate social situations with grace and empathy and build more meaningful and fulfilling relationships. If you find that managing narcissistic tendencies in social settings is overwhelming, seeking support from a mental health professional may be helpful. Remember that managing narcissistic tendencies is a journey, and it requires ongoing attention and effort. By prioritizing self-growth and building meaningful connections with others, we can overcome the challenges of narcissistic tendencies and create a more fulfilling life.

It's also important to recognize that managing narcissistic tendencies is not just an individual responsibility but a collective one. Social settings can often reinforce and amplify narcissistic tendencies, and it's crucial to create a culture of empathy, understanding, and mutual respect. This involves setting norms and expectations for communication and behavior and actively working to develop a sense of safety and belonging for everyone involved.

In addition, it's essential to recognize that narcissistic tendencies can be deeply rooted in cultural and societal norms. For example, in many cultures, self-promotion, and individualism are highly valued, reinforcing narcissistic tendencies and making it difficult to build healthy relationships. By challenging these norms and creating a culture of empathy and understanding, we can break down the barriers to meaningful connections and build a more compassionate and fulfilling society.

Ultimately, managing narcissistic tendencies in social settings requires a commitment to self-growth, empathy, and understanding. By building empathy and compassion, setting healthy boundaries, addressing past experiences and trauma, practicing gratitude and humility, engaging in acts of kindness and generosity, prioritizing self-care and well-being, we can navigate social situations with grace and empathy, and build more meaningful ones and fulfilling relationships. If you find that managing narcissistic tendencies in social settings is overwhelming, seeking support from a mental health professional may be helpful. Remember that managing narcissistic tendencies is a journey, and it requires ongoing attention and effort. By prioritizing self-growth and building meaningful connections with others, we can overcome the challenges of narcissistic tendencies and create a more fulfilling life.

Have you noticed any narcissistic tendencies in social situations? How do these tendencies manifest and impact your interactions with others?

What strategies can you use to manage these tendencies and ensure they don't take over your behavior in social settings?

Reflect on a recent social situation where you successfully managed your narcissistic tendencies. What did you do differently and what was the outcome?

Chapter 7

Seek Professional Help

Seeking professional help can be essential in addressing a range of personal and interpersonal challenges, including mental health issues, relationship difficulties, and substance abuse. This chapter will explore the benefits of seeking professional help, the different types of mental health professionals available, and strategies for finding the proper professional to meet your needs.

One of the primary benefits of seeking professional help is the guidance and support trained mental health professionals provide. Mental health professionals are trained to help individuals navigate various personal and interpersonal challenges, including depression, anxiety, trauma, and addiction. They can provide tools and strategies for coping with difficult emotions and managing challenging situations. In addition, they can offer a safe and confidential space for individuals to explore their thoughts and feelings.

Another benefit of seeking professional help is the sense of validation and support mental health professionals provide. Mental health challenges can often feel isolating and overwhelming, and seeking professional help can give a sense of connection and validation to individuals struggling. Working with a mental health professional makes individuals feel less alone and more supported in their journey toward healing and growth.

In addition to the benefits of seeking professional help, it's essential to recognize that a variety of mental health professionals are available to meet each individual's unique needs. These professionals may include psychologists, psychiatrists, social workers, counselors, and therapists. Each of these professionals brings a fantastic set of skills and training to their work, and it's essential to find the right fit for your individual needs and preferences.

Psychologists are mental health professionals trained to assess, diagnose, and treat various mental health issues. They may specialize in specific areas of mental health, such as anxiety or depression, and can provide a range of evidence-based treatments, including cognitive-behavioral and interpersonal therapy.

Psychiatrists are medical doctors who specialize in diagnosing, treating, and managing mental health issues. They are licensed to prescribe medication and may also provide therapy and counseling services.

Social workers are mental health professionals who specialize in providing social and emotional support to individuals and families. They may work in various settings, including schools, hospitals, and community organizations, and may provide case management, counseling, and advocacy services.

Counselors and therapists are mental health professionals who specialize in providing counseling and therapy services to individuals and families. They may offer a range of evidence-based treatments, including cognitive-behavioral and psychoanalytic therapy, and work in various settings, including private practice, community organizations, and schools.

When seeking professional help, it's essential to consider your individual needs and preferences and the type of mental health professional best suited to meet them. This may involve researching different mental health professionals, requesting recommendations from friends or family, and scheduling consultations or appointments to determine the best fit for your needs.

It's also important to recognize that seeking professional help is a process and may involve multiple sessions or appointments to achieve your desired outcomes. Building a trusting and supportive relationship with your mental health professional takes time and effort but can ultimately lead to positive changes in your life and relationships.

If you are unsure about seeking professional help, contact a mental health hotline or support group for guidance and resources. These resources can provide information and support for individuals who may be struggling with mental health challenges and can help to connect individuals with the right mental health professional to meet their needs.

In addition to seeking professional help, there are some strategies that individuals can use to support their mental health and well-being. These may include engaging in regular exercise and physical activity, practicing mindfulness and meditation, maintaining a healthy diet and sleep routine, and seeking support from friends and family. These strategies can help support overall mental health and well-being and complement the support provided by mental health professionals.

It's also important to recognize that seeking professional help is not a sign of weakness but strength and resilience. Mental health challenges can be overwhelming and difficult to manage on our own, and seeking professional help can provide the guidance and support necessary to move toward healing and growth.

If you are considering seeking professional help, it's essential to approach the process with an open mind and a willingness to explore your thoughts and feelings. This may involve discussing difficult emotions and experiences and require a willingness to be vulnerable and honest with your mental health professional. However, approaching the process with an open mind and a desire to explore can create a safe and supportive environment for personal growth and healing.

In conclusion, seeking professional help can be essential in addressing a range of personal and interpersonal challenges. Working with a mental health professional can provide guidance and support for various mental health issues, including depression, anxiety, trauma, and addiction. When seeking professional help, it's essential to consider your individual needs and preferences and to find the right mental health professional to meet those needs. If you are unsure about seeking professional help, reaching out to a mental health hotline or support group for guidance and resources may be helpful. Ultimately, seeking professional help is a sign of strength and resilience and can provide the advice and support necessary to move toward healing and growth.

In what ways do you believe professional help could benefit you in overcoming narcissism or other personal challenges?

If you have sought professional help in the past, how has it impacted your journey towards self-improvement?

What barriers, if any, do you face when considering seeking professional help? How can you work to overcome them?

Chapter 8

Self-Reflection and Personal Growth

Self-reflection and personal growth are essential components of a fulfilling and meaningful life. By self-reflection, individuals can gain insight into their thoughts, feelings, and behaviors and make significant changes to improve their relationships, work, and overall well-being. This chapter will explore the importance of self-reflection and personal growth and provide strategies for engaging in this process.

Self-reflection involves stepping back from our daily routines and activities and objectively examining our thoughts, feelings, and behaviors. This can include journaling, meditation, or simply reflecting on our experiences and interactions with others. By engaging in self-reflection, we can gain insight into our behavior patterns, motivations, and goals and make meaningful changes to improve our relationships and overall well-being.

One key aspect of self-reflection is identifying and challenging our limiting beliefs and self-talk. Many individuals engage in negative self-talk or hold limiting beliefs about their abilities or worth, which can prevent them from reaching their full potential. By self-reflection, we can identify these limiting beliefs and self-talk and work on challenging and replacing them with more positive and empowering thoughts and ideas.

Another critical aspect of self-reflection is identifying and managing our emotions. Emotions can be powerful and overwhelming, often leading to impulsive or destructive behaviors. By self-reflection, we can gain insight into our emotional triggers and develop strategies for managing our emotions in healthy and productive ways.

Self-reflection can also help us to develop greater self-awareness and empathy towards others. By examining our thoughts, feelings, and behaviors, we can gain a deeper understanding of the experiences and perspectives of others and develop greater empathy and compassion toward them.

In addition to self-reflection, personal growth involves actively seeking new experiences and challenges that help us grow and develop as individuals. This may include pursuing new hobbies or interests, engaging in education or training programs, or seeking new social or professional opportunities.

One key aspect of personal growth is stepping outside our comfort zones and taking risks. By taking on new challenges and experiences, we can develop new skills and perspectives and build greater confidence and resilience in adversity.

Another critical aspect of personal growth is developing healthy and meaningful relationships. Relationships provide an essential source of support and connection and help us navigate life's challenges and achieve our goals. Investing in our relationships and seeking new opportunities for fellowship and support can build a more fulfilling and meaningful life.

To engage in self-reflection and personal growth, it's essential to establish a regular practice or routine. This may involve setting aside time each day or week for journaling, meditation, or other self-reflective activities and seeking out new opportunities for personal growth and development.

It's also essential to approach the process of self-reflection and personal growth with a sense of curiosity and openness. This may involve challenging our preconceived notions and beliefs and being willing to explore new ideas and perspectives.

Finally, it's essential to recognize that self-reflection and personal growth are a journey that may involve setbacks and challenges. However, by approaching the process with patience and self-compassion and seeking support and guidance from others as needed, we can navigate these challenges and continue to grow and develop as individuals.

In conclusion, self-reflection and personal growth are essential to a fulfilling and meaningful life. By self-reflection, we can gain insight into our thoughts, feelings, and behaviors and make significant changes to improve our relationships, work, and overall well-being. By actively seeking new experiences and challenges, we can grow and develop as individuals and build greater confidence and resilience in adversity. By establishing a regular practice of self-reflection and personal growth and approaching the process with curiosity and openness, we can continue to learn, grow, and thrive throughout our lives.

How has self-reflection played a role in your journey to overcome narcissism or other personal challenges?

What insights have you gained about yourself through self-reflection? How can you use these insights to foster personal growth?

How can you make self-reflection a consistent practice in your life to promote ongoing personal development?

Chapter 9

Self-Reflection and Personal Growth

Loving someone who struggles with narcissism can be a challenging and complex experience. Narcissism is a personality disorder characterized by excessive self-importance, a lack of empathy for others, and a preoccupation with power and success. Individuals with narcissistic personality disorder often struggle with maintaining healthy relationships and may exhibit behaviors such as manipulation, lying, and emotional abuse. This chapter will explore strategies for supporting loved ones in overcoming narcissism and building healthy, fulfilling relationships.

One of the most essential strategies for supporting loved ones in overcoming narcissism is to approach the situation with empathy and understanding. Individuals with narcissistic personality disorder often struggle with shame, insecurity, and inadequacy, which can fuel their selfish behaviors. By approaching the situation with compassion and empathy, we can help to create a safe and supportive environment for our loved ones to begin the process of healing and growth.

Another important strategy for supporting loved ones in overcoming narcissism is to set healthy boundaries and expectations. Narcissistic behaviors often involve manipulation, lying, and emotional abuse, damaging our emotional well-being. By setting clear and firm boundaries around these behaviors, we can help protect ourselves and our loved ones from harm while offering support and understanding.

Encouraging our loved ones to seek professional help, such as therapy or counseling, is also essential. Narcissism is a complex and challenging disorder and often requires the guidance and support of a trained mental health professional. By encouraging our loved ones to seek professional help, we can help to create a safe and supportive environment for healing and growth.

In addition to professional help, offering our loved ones emotional support and encouragement is essential. This may involve offering a listening ear, providing emotional validation, or simply being present and available for our loved ones when they need us. By providing emotional support and encouragement, we can help to create a sense of connection and validation for our loved ones and help to build their confidence and self-esteem.

Another important strategy for supporting loved ones in overcoming narcissism is to model healthy relationship behaviors. Narcissistic behaviors often involve a lack of empathy, manipulation, and emotional abuse, which can damage relationships. By modeling healthy and respectful relationship behaviors, we can help to create a supportive and positive environment for our loved ones to learn and grow.

It's essential to recognize that supporting loved ones in overcoming narcissism can be long and challenging and may involve setbacks and challenges. However, by approaching the process with patience and compassion and seeking support and guidance from others as needed, we can navigate these challenges and continue to support our loved ones in their journey toward healing and growth.

A critical aspect of supporting loved ones in overcoming narcissism is to validate their feelings and experiences. Individuals with narcissistic personality disorder often struggle with shame, inadequacy, and a lack of self-worth. By validating their feelings and experiences, we can help create a safe and supportive environment for them to express their emotions and heal.

It's also important to avoid engaging in power struggles or arguments with our loved ones who struggle with narcissism. Narcissistic individuals often seek power and control in their relationships and may become defensive or argumentative when their sense of control is threatened. By avoiding power struggles and arguments, we can help to create a more positive and productive environment for communication and growth.

Another essential aspect of supporting loved ones in overcoming narcissism is encouraging them to practice self-reflection and personal growth. By practicing self-reflection and engaging in personal development, our loved ones can gain insight into their thoughts, feelings, and behaviors and begin to make meaningful changes to improve their relationships and overall well-being. This may involve encouraging our loved ones to seek new experiences and challenges, engage in therapy or counseling, or practice mindfulness and meditation.

In some cases, supporting loved ones in overcoming narcissism may involve making difficult choices or decisions. For example, if a loved one's narcissistic behaviors are consistently harmful or abusive, it may be necessary to establish more strict boundaries or to remove oneself from the relationship entirely. While these decisions can be painful and difficult, they may ultimately be required for the well-being of ourselves and our loved ones.

It's also important to recognize that supporting loved ones in overcoming narcissism may involve significant emotional labor and self-care. We must take care of our emotional well-being as we navigate the challenges and complexities of keeping our loved ones in their journey toward healing and growth. This may involve seeking support and guidance from friends, family, or mental health professionals, practicing self-care activities such as exercise, meditation, or creative pursuits, and setting clear boundaries around our emotional needs and limitations.

In conclusion, supporting loved ones in overcoming narcissism can be challenging but can ultimately lead to healing and growth for both the individual and the relationship. By approaching the situation with empathy and understanding, setting healthy boundaries and expectations, encouraging professional help, offering emotional support and encouragement, modeling healthy relationship behaviors, and practicing self-reflection and personal growth, we can create a supportive and positive environment for our loved ones to learn and grow. It's essential to recognize that supporting loved ones in overcoming narcissism may involve setbacks and challenges, ultimately requiring difficult decisions or choices. However, by approaching the process with patience and compassion and seeking support and guidance from others as needed, we can navigate these challenges and continue to support our loved ones in their journey toward healing and growth.

Chapter 10

Self-Reflection and Personal Growth

Triggers and relapses can be significant challenges for individuals who struggle with narcissism or have loved ones who struggle with selfishness. Triggers are events, situations, or people that can elicit intense emotional reactions or behaviors in individuals with narcissistic tendencies. Relapses refer to a return to previous behavior patterns, often after a period of progress or improvement. Therefore, coping with triggers and relapses is essential to the healing and recovery process. In this chapter, we will explore strategies for dealing with triggers and relapses and maintaining progress and growth toward healing and recovery.

One of the most important strategies for coping with triggers and relapses is to develop a plan of action for when they occur. This may involve identifying specific triggers, such as certain social situations or conversations, and developing strategies for managing those triggers. For example, suppose a particular social situation tends to trigger narcissistic behaviors. In that case, an individual may develop a plan to limit their exposure to that situation or to practice specific coping strategies when they are in that situation.

It is important to remember that everyone's triggers and coping strategies may differ. Some triggers may be specific situations or people, while others may be more abstract, such as feelings of shame or vulnerability. Similarly, coping strategies vary widely, from deep breathing exercises to distraction techniques. Identifying what works best for each individual and tailoring coping strategies to individual needs and experiences is essential.

Another important strategy for coping with triggers and relapses is to engage in self-care activities that promote emotional well-being and stability. This may involve practicing mindfulness and meditation, regular exercise or physical activity, or creative or expressive pursuits. By engaging in self-care activities, individuals can help to build resilience and stability in the face of triggers and relapses and promote overall emotional and mental well-being.

It is also essential to seek support from others during triggers and relapses. This may involve seeking the guidance and support of a therapist or counselor or reaching out to friends or family members for support and encouragement. By seeking out support from others, individuals can help create a sense of connection and validation and build a support system to help them navigate the challenges of triggers and relapses.

Another important strategy for coping with triggers and relapses is to practice self-compassion and forgiveness. Individuals with narcissistic tendencies often struggle with feelings of shame and self-blame, which can fuel their selfish behaviors. By practicing self-compassion and forgiveness, individuals can help to break this cycle of guilt and self-blame and cultivate a more positive and supportive relationship with themselves.

It is essential to recognize that triggers and relapses are a natural part of the healing and recovery process and may occur even after significant progress. By approaching triggers and relapses with patience and compassion and viewing them as opportunities for learning and growth, individuals can continue to progress toward healing and recovery.

Sometimes, coping with triggers and relapses may require changing the environment or social relationships. For example, suppose a particular relationship or social circle consistently triggers narcissistic behaviors. In that case, it may be necessary to limit exposure to those individuals or to seek out more positive and supportive social relationships. While these decisions can be difficult and painful, they may ultimately be necessary for emotional well-being and growth.

It is important to remember that coping with triggers and relapses can be challenging, but it is an essential part of the healing and recovery journey. By developing a plan of action for managing triggers, engaging in self-care activities, seeking out support from others, practicing self-compassion and forgiveness, and making necessary changes to the environment or social relationships, individuals can build resilience and stability in the face of triggers and relapses, and continue to make progress on the path towards healing and recovery. It is also essential to recognize that triggers and relapses can be opportunities for learning and growth, ultimately leading to greater emotional and mental well-being.

One strategy for coping with triggers and relapses is to practice mindfulness. Mindfulness involves bringing one's attention to the present moment without judgment. By practicing mindfulness, individuals can learn to become more aware of their thoughts, emotions, and behaviors. As a result, they can learn to respond to triggers and relapses more deliberately.

Another strategy for coping with triggers and relapses is to practice self-reflection. Self-reflection involves reflecting on one's thoughts, feelings, and behaviors and identifying patterns or triggers contributing to narcissistic behaviors. By practicing self-reflection, individuals can better understand themselves and their motivations and develop more effective coping strategies.

In addition to these strategies, individuals must remain committed to their healing and recovery journey, despite setbacks and challenges. This may involve setting achievable goals, celebrating progress and achievements, and recognizing that setbacks and relapses are a natural part of the healing process. By remaining committed to their journey, individuals can continue progressing and growing, even in the face of obstacles.

Finally, it is essential to recognize that coping with triggers and relapses may require professional help. Therapists and counselors can provide guidance and support and help individuals develop effective coping strategies for managing triggers and relapses. Additionally, therapists can help individuals to build a better understanding of themselves and their triggers and can help them to develop more effective communication and relationship skills.

In conclusion, coping with triggers and relapses is essential to the healing and recovery journey for individuals who struggle with narcissism or have loved ones who work with narcissism. By developing a plan of action for managing triggers, engaging in self-care activities, seeking out support from others, practicing self-compassion and forgiveness, and remaining committed to the healing journey, individuals can build resilience and stability in the face of triggers and relapses and continue to make progress on the path towards healing and recovery. While coping with triggers and relapses can be challenging, it is essential to remember that they are a natural part of the healing process and can ultimately lead to greater emotional and mental well-being.

Book 2

Breaking the Cycle of Compulsive Lying

Chapter 1

The Psychology of Lying

Lying is an expected behavior that can significantly affect personal and professional relationships. Individuals who struggle with compulsive lying may experience shame, guilt, and anxiety and work to maintain positive and healthy relationships. This chapter will explore the psychology of lying and the underlying motivations and factors that contribute to compulsive lying behaviors.

Lying can take many forms, from minor white lies to more significant and damaging falsehoods. Sometimes, lying may be motivated by a desire to protect oneself or others from harm or punishment. For example, someone may lie to avoid being blamed for a mistake or watch a loved one from criticism. In other cases, lying may be motivated by a desire to gain social status or acceptance. For example, someone may lie about their accomplishments or experiences to impress others or fit in with a particular social group.

In addition to these motivations, several psychological factors can contribute to compulsive lying behaviors. One factor is a lack of self-esteem or self-worth. Individuals with low self-esteem may lie to present a more favorable image of themselves to others. This can lead to a cycle of lying behaviors, as the individual seeks to maintain the false impression they have created.

Another psychological factor contributing to lying behaviors is a lack of empathy or consideration for others. For example, individuals who struggle with their hearts may be more likely to lie to avoid the negative emotions or reactions of others. Additionally, individuals who have difficulty considering the needs and feelings of others may be more likely to lie to gain personal advantages or to avoid negative consequences. It is also essential to recognize that compulsive lying can be a symptom of underlying mental health conditions, such as borderline or narcissistic personality disorder. These conditions can contribute to challenging behaviors, including compulsive lying, and may require professional treatment.

Despite the negative consequences of lying, individuals who struggle with compulsive lying may find it difficult to stop. Lying can become a habitual behavior challenging to break, particularly if it has been reinforced by favorable outcomes in the past. Additionally, individuals who struggle with compulsive lying may experience feelings of shame or guilt, which can contribute to further lying behaviors.

One strategy for addressing compulsive lying is identifying the underlying motivations and factors contributing to the behavior. By understanding the reasons behind lying behaviors, individuals can develop strategies for managing those motivations and addressing the underlying psychological factors. For example, if lying is motivated by a desire to gain social acceptance, an individual may focus on building healthier and more positive relationships based on honesty and authenticity.

Another strategy for addressing compulsive lying is to practice self-reflection and self-awareness. By becoming more aware of one's thoughts and behaviors, individuals can identify patterns of deception and develop strategies for managing those patterns. Additionally, by practicing self-reflection, individuals can create more positive and healthy self-esteem, which can help reduce the need for lying behaviors.

It is also essential to seek out professional help for compulsive lying behaviors. Therapists and counselors can provide guidance and support and help individuals develop effective coping strategies for managing lying behaviors. Additionally, therapists can help individuals build a better understanding of themselves and their motivations and provide support and guidance as they work towards positive changes in their behavior.

In conclusion, the psychology of lying is a complex and multifaceted topic, with various underlying motivations and factors contributing to compulsive lying behaviors. While lying can have significant negative consequences in personal and professional relationships, it is possible to address and manage compulsive lying behaviors with the right strategies and support. By identifying the underlying motivations and factors contributing to lying behaviors, practicing self-reflection and self-awareness, and seeking professional help, individuals can develop effective strategies for managing lying behaviors and build healthier, more positive relationships based on honesty and authenticity. While addressing compulsive lying can be challenging, it is an essential part of the journey toward personal growth and healing. It can ultimately lead to greater emotional and mental well-being.

Chapter 2

Facing the Truth

Facing the truth about oneself can be one of the most challenging and uncomfortable aspects of personal growth and self-improvement. However, it is essential to healing, developing, and becoming the best version of oneself. This chapter will explore the importance of facing the truth, strategies for approaching this process honestly and with self-compassion, and the benefits of acknowledging brutal facts.

One of the primary reasons why facing the truth can be so challenging is that it requires individuals to confront aspects of themselves or their lives that they may have been avoiding or denying. This may involve acknowledging past mistakes or regrets, recognizing negative patterns of behavior, or accepting uncomfortable truths about personal relationships or situations. It may also include confronting difficult emotions like shame, guilt, or fear.

It is an essential step toward personal growth and healing despite the discomfort of facing the truth. By acknowledging and accepting brutal facts about oneself, individuals can begin to address underlying issues or challenges and develop effective strategies for making positive changes in their lives. Additionally, facing the truth can help individuals develop more positive and healthy self-esteem based on honesty and authenticity.

One effective strategy for facing the truth is to approach the process with self-compassion. This means recognizing that facing reality can be challenging and uncomfortable and practicing self-care activities to support oneself. For example, individuals may choose to engage in relaxing activities such as meditation or yoga or seek the support of loved ones or a professional therapist. Writing down thoughts and feelings about the truth being faced can also help in processing and reflecting on experiences in a non-judgmental way.

Another strategy for facing the truth is to focus on the present moment instead of dwelling on past mistakes or regrets. While it's important to acknowledge past mistakes and negative behaviors, it's crucial to focus on developing effective strategies for making positive changes in the present. For example, suppose an individual recognizes that they have a pattern of being dishonest in personal relationships. In that case, they may focus on building healthier and more positive relationships based on honesty and authenticity.

It's essential to recognize that facing the truth is an ongoing process, not a one-time event. Individuals may need to revisit and re-examine brutal facts about themselves or their lives as they grow and develop. They may also need professional help, such as therapy or counseling, to address underlying issues or challenges in facing the truth.

One of the benefits of facing the truth is that it can lead to personal growth and development. By acknowledging brutal truths, individuals can work on improving negative patterns of behavior, which can lead to greater emotional and mental well-being. Additionally, facing reality can help individuals build more robust, positive relationships based on honesty and authenticity. When we are honest with ourselves, we can be more open with others, leading to deeper and more meaningful connections.

Another benefit of facing the truth is that it can lead to increased self-awareness. Individuals can better understand their motivations, values, and needs by acknowledging and accepting brutal facts about themselves. This increased self-awareness can help individuals make more informed decisions about their lives, including personal and professional relationships.

Lastly, facing the truth can lead to a greater sense of purpose and direction in life. When individuals are honest about their strengths, weaknesses, and aspirations, they can set realistic goals and take meaningful action toward achieving them. By acknowledging brutal truths, individuals can work towards becoming the best version of themselves and living a more fulfilling life.

In conclusion, facing the truth about oneself or one's life can be difficult and uncomfortable, but it is an essential step toward personal growth and healing. By acknowledging and accepting brutal truths, individuals can address underlying issues or challenges, develop effective strategies for making positive changes, and build more significant and positive relationships based on honesty and authenticity. While facing the truth can be an ongoing process, it can lead to increased self-awareness, greater emotional and mental well-being, and a greater sense of purpose and direction in life. By approaching the process with honesty, self-compassion, and a willingness to seek professional help, individuals can navigate the challenges of facing the truth and emerge more robust and resilient on the other side.

Chapter 3

Rebuilding Trust and Credibility

Building trust and credibility is critical to any healthy, personal, or professional relationship. However, repairing damage to a relationship can be challenging and complex, and rebuilding trust and credibility can take time and effort. This chapter will explore the importance of rebuilding trust and credibility and strategies for approaching this process with honesty, openness, and compassion.

The first step in rebuilding trust and credibility is acknowledging the harm caused. This means taking responsibility for the actions or behaviors that led to the loss of confidence or credibility and expressing genuine remorse and apology for the damage that has been caused. Acknowledging the impact of the actions or behaviors and expressing a sincere desire to make things right is crucial.

Another critical step in rebuilding trust and credibility is to be open and transparent about the situation. This means being willing to answer questions, provide information as needed, and listen to concerns and feedback from the other person. Again, it is essential to be honest and upfront about relevant news and avoid withholding or hiding critical details.

In addition to being open and transparent, it is crucial to take concrete steps to address the situation and prevent similar problems from occurring in the future. This may involve implementing new policies or procedures, seeking professional help, or changing behavior or mindset. Demonstrating a commitment to making positive changes and taking responsibility for one's actions is essential.

Consistency and reliability over time are also critical aspects of rebuilding trust and credibility. This means following through on commitments, being punctual and dependable, and being willing to be accountable for one's actions. Demonstrating a sustained effort to make positive changes and rebuild the relationship is essential.

It is also essential to recognize that rebuilding trust and credibility takes time and effort and may not happen overnight. Therefore, it is crucial to be patient and understanding and to demonstrate a commitment to the process over the long term. This may involve regular check-ins or follow-up conversations and a willingness to listen and respond to concerns or feedback.

When working to rebuild trust and credibility, it is essential to be mindful of the impact of one's actions on the other person. This means being empathetic and compassionate and working to understand the other person's perspective and feelings. In addition, it is essential to approach the situation with an open mind and a willingness to learn and grow.

In some cases, rebuilding trust and credibility may not be possible, and the relationship may need to end or be redefined. Therefore, it is essential to make a sincere effort to repair the damage and rebuild the relationship. Still, it is also necessary to be realistic about the outcome and to prioritize one's own well-being and emotional health.

Seeking out support from others can help rebuild trust and credibility. Whether it be a trusted friend or family member, a professional therapist, or a support group, talking through the situation and feelings with others can help provide perspective, validation, and encouragement and help individuals feel less isolated and alone.

Practicing self-care and self-compassion while rebuilding trust and credibility is also critical. This means engaging in activities that promote emotional and mental well-being, such as exercise, meditation, or spending time with loved ones. It also means being kind and forgiving towards oneself and recognizing that making mistakes and facing challenges are a normal part of the human experience.

In addition to practicing self-care and seeking out support from others, it can be helpful to practice gratitude and appreciation for the positive aspects of the relationship. This means focusing on the positive qualities and experiences within the relationship and expressing gratitude and appreciation for these aspects. This helps cultivate a positive and supportive environment for rebuilding trust and credibility.

In conclusion, rebuilding trust and credibility is essential to repairing damaged relationships, whether personal or professional. By acknowledging the harm caused, being open and transparent, taking concrete steps to address the situation, and demonstrating consistency and reliability over time, it is possible to rebuild trust and credibility and restore relationships to a healthy and positive state. While the process may be challenging and take time, with patience, understanding, and commitment, moving forward and rebuilding more robust, more resilient relationships based on honesty, openness, and compassion is possible.

Rebuilding trust and credibility requires significant time and effort, but the benefits of doing so are immense. By repairing damaged relationships, individuals can experience greater emotional connection, fulfillment, and overall well-being. In addition, improving damaged relationships can help to promote healthy communication, resolve conflicts, and create a more positive and supportive environment for all involved.

While rebuilding trust and credibility may seem daunting, it is essential to remember that it is a process and that progress may be slow and incremental. Individuals can gradually rebuild trust and credibility over time by focusing on the present moment and taking small, consistent steps toward positive change. With patience, dedication, and a willingness to learn and grow, individuals can repair damaged relationships and build stronger, more fulfilling connections with others.

Chapter 4

Identifying the Underlying Causes of Lying

Lying is a behavior that can cause significant harm to relationships and overall well-being. Understanding why someone may lie can be challenging, but identifying the underlying causes can be a critical step in addressing and overcoming the behavior. This chapter will explore some common underlying causes of lying and strategies for identifying and managing them.

One common cause of lying is fear. People may lie to avoid punishment, rejection, or adverse consequences. This fear may stem from past experiences or learned behavior and may be reinforced by the belief that lying is the only way to avoid negative outcomes. It is essential to recognize that while lying may temporarily relieve fear or anxiety, it can lead to feelings of guilt, shame, and decreased trust in relationships over time.

Another common cause of lying is low self-esteem. People with low self-esteem may need to present themselves in a certain way or avoid appearing vulnerable or imperfect. This may lead them to exaggerate their accomplishments or lie about their experiences or abilities. Lying in this context may be a way of coping with feelings of inadequacy or insecurity, and addressing these underlying issues can help reduce the need to lie.

A third common cause of lying is a desire for attention or approval. People may lie to gain recognition or admiration from others or avoid disapproval or criticism. This may stem from a need for validation or a fear of rejection and may be reinforced by social or cultural norms prioritizing achievement or success. It is essential to recognize that while lying in this context may initially provide a sense of validation, it may ultimately lead to feelings of emptiness or disconnection, and seeking validation from external sources may not provide a sustainable source of happiness or fulfillment.

To identify the underlying causes of lying, reflecting on the context in which it occurs can be helpful. This may involve examining the situations or triggers that lead to lying and the thoughts and emotions that arise in these situations. It can also be beneficial to reflect on past experiences or learned behavior that may contribute to the behavior.

Another helpful strategy for identifying the underlying causes of lying is to seek out feedback and perspective from others. This may involve talking to trusted friends or family members, seeking professional therapy, or joining a support group for people struggling with lying. By opening up about the behavior and seeking support and guidance, individuals can understand the underlying causes and develop strategies for addressing the behavior.

Addressing the underlying causes of lying may involve a range of strategies, depending on the individual and the situation. For example, individuals who lie out of fear may benefit from developing healthy coping mechanisms for dealing with anxiety or stress, such as exercise, mindfulness, or therapy. Those who lie due to low self-esteem may benefit from building self-confidence and self-acceptance through positive self-talk or affirmations. Those who lie for attention or approval may benefit from developing healthy relationships based on authenticity and mutual support rather than external validation.

It is essential to recognize that addressing the underlying causes of lying may take time and effort and that progress may be slow and incremental. It is also crucial to be patient and compassionate and recognize that overcoming the behavior is a journey rather than a destination. Seeking support and guidance from others can be an essential part of this process, as can practicing self-care and self-compassion throughout the journey.

It is essential to note that while identifying the underlying causes of lying is important, taking responsibility for the behavior and its impact on others is also crucial. This involves acknowledging the harm caused by lying, making amends where possible, and committing to positive changes.

In conclusion, identifying the underlying causes of lying is essential to addressing and overcoming the behavior. Fear, low self-esteem, and a desire for attention or approval are common underlying causes of lying, but there may be others. By reflecting on the context in which lying occurs and seeking support and guidance, individuals can gain insight into the root causes of their behavior and develop strategies for making positive changes.

It is important to note that addressing the underlying causes of lying is not a one-size-fits-all approach. Different individuals may have other underlying reasons for their lying behavior, and different strategies may be needed to address these causes. Therefore, seeking professional help, such as therapy or counseling, is crucial to identify and address the underlying causes of lying.

One common strategy used in therapy is cognitive-behavioral therapy (CBT), a form of talk therapy that focuses on changing negative thoughts and behaviors. CBT can help individuals identify the underlying beliefs and thought patterns contributing to their lying behavior and develop alternative, more positive ways of thinking and behaving. Other therapeutic approaches that may help address lying behavior include dialectical behavior therapy (DBT), mindfulness-based therapy, and family therapy.

In addition to seeking out professional help, there are also several self-help strategies that individuals can use to address their lying behavior. One helpful approach is to keep a journal, where individuals can reflect on the situations that trigger their lying behavior and their thoughts and emotions in these situations. This can help individuals gain insight into the underlying causes of their behavior and develop alternative, more positive ways of responding to these situations.

Another helpful self-help strategy is to practice self-compassion. Lying can often be accompanied by guilt and shame, making it difficult to break the cycle of lying. Self-compassion involves treating oneself with kindness, understanding, and acceptance rather than self-criticism and judgment. This can help individuals develop a more positive self-image and reduce the need to lie.

It is also essential to develop healthy communication skills in relationships. This involves being honest and transparent with others, even when difficult or uncomfortable. Healthy communication skills also involve active listening, empathy, and respecting the boundaries and needs of others. By developing these skills, individuals can build trust and intimacy in relationships and reduce the need to lie.

Chapter 5

Strategies for Coping With Stress and Anxiety

Stress and anxiety are everyday experiences in our daily lives. While some stress is everyday, chronic stress can harm physical and mental health. Additionally, anxiety can lead to excessive worry, panic, and avoidance behaviors that interfere with our daily functioning. Therefore, learning effective coping strategies to manage stress and anxiety is essential.

There are numerous ways to cope with stress and anxiety, and not every strategy works for everyone. However, some of the effective coping strategies include:

1. Mindfulness meditation involves focusing on the present moment and observing thoughts and feelings without judgment. By practicing mindfulness, individuals can reduce stress and anxiety by improving emotional regulation, increasing self-awareness, and promoting relaxation. It can be practiced anywhere; even a

few minutes of mindfulness meditation daily can make a significant difference.

2. Physical exercise: Exercise releases endorphins, natural mood enhancers that can improve sleep quality, increase energy, and reduce symptoms of anxiety and depression. Regular exercise can also be an outlet for emotional energy, which can help individuals manage stress and anxiety. Additionally, exercise can be a social activity, which can provide an additional source of support and stress relief.

3. Relaxation techniques: There are various relaxation techniques, such as deep breathing exercises, progressive muscle relaxation, and visualization. These techniques can help individuals reduce physical tension, calm their minds, and reduce the emotional and physical symptoms of stress and anxiety. Finding a relaxation technique that works best for an individual is essential.

4. Engaging in hobbies or activities: Engaging in enjoyable activities such as spending time with loved ones, pursuing interests, or engaging in creative activities can provide a sense of purpose and fulfillment and distract from stress and anxiety. Setting aside time for these activities is crucial as they can help individuals recharge and refocus.

5. Setting realistic goals: Breaking down larger goals into smaller, manageable steps can help individuals gain a sense of accomplishment and reduce overwhelming feelings. Additionally,

prioritizing self-care activities, such as getting enough sleep, eating well, and engaging in regular physical activity, can help individuals better manage their stress and anxiety levels.

6. Seeking professional help: Seeking professional help, such as therapy or counseling, can provide individuals with the tools and support they need to manage their stress and anxiety levels and improve their overall well-being. A mental health professional can work with individuals to develop a personalized treatment plan that addresses their specific needs.

It's important to remember that coping with stress and anxiety is a process that takes time and effort. It is also essential to seek help if stress and anxiety interfere with daily life. Here are some additional tips that can help individuals cope with stress and anxiety:

- Practice self-compassion and be kind to yourself
- Stay connected with supportive friends and family members
- Avoid self-medicating with alcohol or drugs
- Take breaks from social media and news
- Get enough sleep, eat a healthy diet, and exercise regularly
- Practice positive thinking and gratitude

Several other techniques can help individuals cope with stress and anxiety. One of these techniques is cognitive-behavioral therapy (CBT). CBT is a therapy that focuses on identifying and changing negative thought patterns that contribute to stress and anxiety. CBT can help individuals develop coping skills, problem-solving strategies, and relaxation techniques to manage stress and anxiety.

Another technique that can help individuals cope with stress and anxiety is expressive writing. Expressive writing involves writing about thoughts and feelings about a stressful or traumatic event. Research has shown that expressive writing can help individuals process their emotions, reduce stress and anxiety, and improve their well-being.

Another technique is the practice of gratitude. Gratitude involves focusing on the positive aspects of one's life and being thankful for them. By practicing gratitude, individuals can shift their focus away from negative thoughts and emotions and improve their mood and well-being. Gratitude can be practiced through journaling, meditation, or simply reflecting on what one is thankful for.

It is important to note that coping with stress and anxiety is not a one-size-fits-all solution. What works for one person may not work for another, and finding the most effective coping strategies may take some time. It is also essential to seek professional help if stress and anxiety become too overwhelming or interfere with daily life.

In conclusion, coping with stress and anxiety is essential to maintaining good mental health. Mindfulness meditation, physical exercise, relaxation techniques, engaging in hobbies or activities, setting realistic goals, and seeking professional help are all effective coping strategies for managing stress and anxiety. Techniques such as cognitive-behavioral therapy, expressive writing, and gratitude can also be helpful. By incorporating these strategies into their daily lives, individuals can reduce the impact of stress and anxiety on their lives and improve their overall well-being.

Chapter 6

Nurturing Honesty in Relationships

Honesty is one of the most crucial aspects of building and maintaining healthy relationships. However, honesty can sometimes be complex, mainly when admitting mistakes or sharing brutal truths. This chapter will discuss nurturing openness in relationships and building strong, lasting connections.

1. Communication is the foundation of building trust and honesty in any relationship. Communicating clearly, openly, and honestly with oneself and others is essential. This involves expressing oneself authentically, actively listening to others, and being willing to compromise and negotiate to reach a mutual understanding. Individuals can build deeper connections and foster more meaningful relationships by prioritizing open and honest communication.

2. Honesty: Being honest with oneself is the first step towards being honest with others. It involves acknowledging and accepting one's thoughts, feelings, and behaviors. It also means taking responsibility for one's actions and being accountable for one's mistakes. By being honest with themselves, individuals can develop a deeper understanding of their values, beliefs, and needs, which can inform how they interact with others in their relationships.

3. Understanding the consequences of dishonesty: It is essential to understand the impact of deception on oneself and others. Being dishonest can damage relationships, undermine trust, and lead to feelings of guilt and shame. It is crucial to recognize that being honest, even when it is difficult, is essential for maintaining healthy relationships. Individuals can build stronger, more resilient relationships based on trust and authenticity by prioritizing honesty.

4. Practice vulnerability: Vulnerability involves being open and honest about one's thoughts and feelings, even when uncomfortable. It can be challenging to open up to others, but it is necessary for building deeper connections and fostering intimacy. By practicing vulnerability, individuals can create a safe and supportive space for themselves and their partners to share their thoughts and feelings openly and honestly.

5. Be willing to apologize and make amends: Apologizing and making amends when one has been dishonest is crucial for repairing

relationships. This involves taking responsibility for one's actions, expressing remorse, and trying to make things right. By being willing to apologize and make amends, individuals can demonstrate their commitment to honesty and repair any damage that may have been done to the relationship.

6. Set clear expectations and boundaries: In relationships, setting clear expectations and boundaries can help prevent dishonesty and promote open communication. It involves discussing one's values, goals, and borders with others and ensuring everyone is on the same page. By setting clear expectations and boundaries, individuals can ensure that they are communicating honestly and transparently with their partners.

7. Seek professional help: If one struggles with being honest or maintaining healthy relationships, it may be helpful to seek professional help. Therapy or counseling can provide individuals with the tools and support to address underlying issues and develop healthy communication and relationship skills. By seeking professional help, individuals can better understand themselves and their relationships and develop the skills they need to build and maintain healthy connections.

8. Practice active listening: Active listening is critical to open and honest communication. It involves entirely focusing on what the other person is saying without interruption or

judgment. By practicing active listening, individuals can demonstrate their commitment to understanding and supporting their partners, which can help build trust and foster more meaningful relationships.

9. Recognize and address patterns of dishonesty: Sometimes, individuals may find themselves falling into patterns of deception in their relationships. These patterns may be rooted in fear, insecurity, or other underlying issues. By recognizing and addressing these patterns, individuals can break the dishonesty cycle and cultivate healthier communication habits.

10. Celebrate honesty: Finally, it is essential to celebrate openness in relationships. When honest with themselves and others, they demonstrate their commitment to building solid and lasting connections based on trust and authenticity. By celebrating honesty, individuals can reinforce the importance of honesty in their relationships and create a supportive and affirming environment for themselves and their partners.

Nurturing honesty in relationships is crucial to building and maintaining healthy connections. By prioritizing open and honest communication, practicing vulnerability, setting clear expectations and boundaries, and seeking professional help, individuals can develop the skills to build solid and lasting connections based on trust and authenticity. In addition, by celebrating honesty and recognizing its positive impact on their relationships, individuals can continue to cultivate healthy communication habits and deepen their connections with their partners.

94

Chapter 7

Mindfulness and Living in the Present Moment

In today's fast-paced world, it's easy to get caught up in the chaos and lose sight of what's truly important. Our minds constantly race, and we often find ourselves distracted by worries, fears, and regrets. This can lead to a sense of stress and overwhelm and a feeling of disconnection from ourselves and the world around us. Mindfulness offers a powerful antidote to this by helping us cultivate a greater sense of presence, awareness, and peace. In this chapter, we will explore the importance of mindfulness and offer tips for growing a mindful approach to life.

1. Understand the benefits of mindfulness: One of the first steps in cultivating mindfulness is understanding its benefits. Research has shown that mindfulness can positively impact both mental and physical health, including reducing

stress and anxiety, improving sleep, and increasing feelings of happiness and well-being. By understanding the benefits of mindfulness, individuals can become more motivated to incorporate it into their daily lives.

2. Practice mindfulness meditation: One of the most popular ways to cultivate mindfulness is through mindfulness meditation. This involves sitting quietly and focusing on the present moment without judgment or distraction. By practicing mindfulness meditation regularly, individuals can train their minds to become more focused and present, which can benefit their mental and emotional well-being. It's important to note that mindfulness meditation is not about stopping thoughts or emptying the mind. Instead, it's about noticing thoughts as they arise, without getting caught up in them, and gently returning the focus to the present moment.

3. Practice mindfulness in everyday activities: Mindfulness does not have to be limited to meditation. It can also be practiced in daily activities, such as eating, walking, or washing dishes. By approaching these activities with a mindful attitude, individuals can bring greater awareness and presence to their daily lives. For example, when eating, one can pay attention to the food's flavors, textures, and sensations rather than mindlessly gobbling it down.

4. Practice self-compassion: Mindfulness involves approaching one's thoughts and feelings with curiosity and openness rather than judgment or

criticism. This also includes practicing self-compassion, which consists in being kind and understanding towards oneself, even in the face of difficulties or challenges. By practicing self-compassion, individuals can cultivate a greater sense of acceptance and peace, which can help them approach life with more mindfulness and presence.

5. Let go of distractions: Mindfulness involves focusing on the present moment rather than getting caught up in distractions or worries. This can be challenging in today's world, where so many distractions are vying for our attention. By letting go of distractions and focusing on the present moment, individuals can cultivate a greater sense of mindfulness and presence in their daily lives. For example, when spending time with loved ones, one can put away their phone and be fully present with them without the distraction of notifications and social media.

6. Practicing gratitude involves cultivating a sense of appreciation for the present moment and the good things in one's life. By focusing on what one is grateful for, individuals can produce a greater sense of mindfulness and presence and positive emotions such as happiness and contentment. This can be done by keeping a gratitude journal or expressing gratitude to others.

7. Seek out mindful activities: Many activities can help individuals cultivate mindfulness, such as yoga, tai chi, or even coloring. By seeking out

these activities and incorporating them into one's routines, individuals can produce a greater sense of mindfulness and presence in their daily lives.

8. Practice mindfulness in relationships: Mindfulness can also be practiced by being fully present with loved ones and approaching communication with curiosity and openness. This can involve active listening, being fully present in conversations, and approaching conflicts with a non-judgmental attitude. By cultivating mindfulness in relationships, individuals can deepen their connections with others and improve the quality of their interactions.

9. Stay committed to mindfulness practice: Cultivating mindfulness is a lifelong journey, and staying committed to the rule is essential, even when it feels challenging. This can involve setting aside time each day for meditation or mindfulness exercises and finding ways to incorporate mindfulness into daily activities. By staying committed to mindfulness, individuals can continue cultivating a greater sense of presence, awareness, and peace in their lives.

Mindfulness is a powerful tool for cultivating a greater sense of presence, awareness, and peace. By understanding its benefits, practicing mindfulness meditation, incorporating mindfulness into daily activities, practicing self-compassion, letting go of distractions, practicing gratitude, seeking out mindful activities, practicing mindfulness in relationships, and staying committed to mindfulness practice, individuals can cultivate a greater sense of mindfulness and presence in their daily lives. Doing so can reduce stress and anxiety, improve mental and physical health, and deepen their connections with themselves and others.

Chapter 8

Seeking Professional Help for Compulsive Lying

Compulsive lying can have significant negative consequences on an individual's life, including damaged relationships, legal issues, and decreased personal and professional integrity. For individuals struggling with compulsive lying, seeking professional help can be crucial in breaking the pattern of behavior and developing healthier habits.

The first step in seeking professional help for compulsive lying is recognizing the signs and admitting that there is a problem. Some symptoms of compulsive lying include lying about even minor details, feeling the compulsion to lie even when it is not necessary, and feeling guilty or ashamed about lying. Once an individual recognizes that they have a problem with compulsive lying, seeking professional help can provide them with the tools and support needed to address the underlying causes of their behavior.

One effective form of professional help for compulsive lying is therapy. Therapy can offer individuals a safe and supportive environment to explore the underlying causes of their lying behavior. Through treatment, individuals can identify co-occurring mental health conditions, such as anxiety or depression, contributing to their lying behavior. Therapy can also help individuals develop healthy coping strategies, such as relaxation techniques or mindfulness practices, to manage the urge to lie.

When seeking professional help for compulsive lying, it is essential to find a therapist who is experienced in treating compulsive lying and who can provide a safe and supportive environment for individuals to explore the underlying causes of their behavior. Researching therapists in the area, asking for referrals from friends or family members, or contacting a mental health organization for recommendations can help individuals find the right therapist for their needs.

To make therapy effective, individuals must be honest and open with their therapist about their lying. This may involve discussing past experiences that may have contributed to their lying behavior and any fears or anxieties about addressing their problem. By being honest and open, individuals can work with their therapist to develop a personalized treatment plan that meets their unique needs.

Therapy can also help individuals better understand themselves and their motivations for lying. This may involve exploring past experiences or trauma contributing to developing their lying behavior. Through this process, individuals can learn to identify triggers and develop strategies for managing compulsive lying tendencies.

Recovery from compulsive lying takes time and patience and involving loved ones in the recovery process can provide individuals with the support and encouragement they need to stay motivated. This may include attending therapy sessions together or seeking help from a support group for families and loved ones of those with compulsive lying.

In addition to therapy, other forms of professional help may be helpful for individuals struggling with compulsive lying. This may include medication for co-occurring mental health conditions or lifestyle changes, such as improved nutrition and exercise habits.

Individuals must remember that recovery from compulsive lying is a gradual process and that setbacks may occur. However, with the help of professional support, individuals can develop the skills and strategies needed to overcome their lying behavior and build more honest and fulfilling relationships.

It is also essential for individuals to be patient with themselves as they work toward recovery. Overcoming compulsive lying is challenging, and it can take time to change deeply ingrained behavior patterns. Individuals should celebrate their progress and not get discouraged by setbacks or relapses.

In addition to seeking professional help, there are also steps individuals can take on their own to support their recovery from compulsive lying. This may include practicing mindfulness and meditation, regular exercise and physical activity, and engaging in activities that bring them joy and fulfillment. In addition, by prioritizing self-care and managing stress and anxiety, individuals can improve their overall mental health and well-being, supporting their recovery from compulsive lying.

Individuals must remember that seeking professional help for compulsive lying is a sign of strength, not weakness. It takes courage to admit that there is a problem and to take steps to address it. With the support of a therapist or counselor, loved ones, and a commitment to personal growth and change, individuals can overcome their lying behavior and build healthier, more fulfilling relationships.

In conclusion, seeking professional help for compulsive lying is crucial for recovery. By recognizing the signs of compulsive lying, finding the right therapist or counselor, being honest and open in therapy, developing healthy coping strategies, addressing co-occurring mental health conditions, involving loved ones in the recovery process, and staying patient and persistent, individuals can overcome compulsive lying and develop healthier patterns of behavior.

Chapter 9

Supporting Loved Ones Struggling with Honesty

When a loved one struggles with honesty, knowing how to support them can be difficult. It can be painful to witness someone we care about repeatedly deceive others and themselves, and it can be challenging to confront them about their behavior without damaging the relationship. However, there are steps individuals can take to support loved ones struggling with honesty.

The first step in supporting a loved one struggling with honesty is approaching the situation with compassion and empathy. Becoming angry or frustrated with a loved one who repeatedly lies can be tempting. Still, it is essential to remember that lying is often rooted in deeper emotional or psychological issues. By approaching the situation with empathy, individuals can create a safe and supportive environment for their loved ones to open up about their struggles with honesty.

One effective way to support a loved one struggling with honesty is to encourage them to seek professional help. This may involve researching therapists in the area who specialize in treating compulsive lying or encouraging them to attend a support group for individuals struggling with honesty. By enabling a loved one to seek professional help, individuals can provide the tools and support they need to break the pattern of dishonesty and develop healthier habits.

It is also essential for individuals to set clear boundaries with loved ones struggling with honesty. This may involve establishing consequences for lying behavior, such as ending a conversation or leaving the room when a loved one begins to lie. While setting boundaries can be challenging, it is crucial for individuals to prioritize their own mental and emotional well-being and not to enable their loved one's lying behavior.

When setting boundaries, it is crucial to do so clearly and compassionately. This may involve explaining to the loved one why the behavior is hurtful and how it affects the relationship. By being honest and transparent, individuals can help their loved ones understand the impact of their behavior and encourage them to take steps to address it.

It is also vital for individuals to listen to their loved ones' concerns and struggles with honesty without judgment or criticism. This may involve asking open-ended questions like "Can you tell me more about why you feel the need to lie?" or "What do you think triggers your lying behavior?" By listening with empathy and understanding, individuals can help their loved ones feel heard and supported, which can, in turn, encourage them to be more honest and open.

In addition to encouraging loved ones to seek professional help and setting boundaries, there are other steps individuals can take to support loved ones struggling with honesty. This may include practicing active listening, expressing gratitude and appreciation for honesty when it does occur, and providing a safe and supportive environment for their loved ones to share their struggles with honesty.

Individuals must remember that supporting a loved one struggling with honesty is challenging and ongoing. It can take time for loved ones to break the pattern of dishonesty and develop healthier habits, and setbacks may occur along the way. However, by approaching the situation with empathy and understanding, encouraging loved ones to seek professional help, setting clear boundaries, and providing a supportive environment for honesty, individuals can help their loved ones overcome their struggles with honesty and build healthier, more fulfilling relationships.

Supporting a loved one struggling with honesty can be challenging, but it is an essential step toward helping them overcome their struggles and build healthier behavior patterns. By approaching the situation with empathy and understanding, encouraging loved ones to seek professional help, setting clear boundaries, and providing a supportive environment for honesty, individuals can support their loved one's journey towards openness and personal growth.

It is also essential for individuals to recognize that supporting a loved one struggling with honesty may be emotionally taxing. It is common for individuals to feel frustrated, hurt, or angry when a loved one repeatedly lies. Therefore, individuals need to prioritize their own mental and emotional well-being. This may involve seeking support from friends or a therapist, engaging in self-care activities, and taking breaks when needed.

In addition to supporting loved ones struggling with honesty, it is also essential for individuals to reflect on their relationship with honesty. This may involve exploring any patterns of dishonesty or mistrust in their relationships and taking steps to address these patterns. By modeling honesty and transparency in their relationships, individuals can set a positive example for their loved ones and encourage healthy habits of communication and trust.

Ultimately, supporting loved ones struggling with honesty requires patience, compassion, and a commitment to personal growth and change. By providing a safe and supportive environment for honesty, encouraging loved ones to seek professional help, and setting clear boundaries, individuals can help their loved ones overcome their struggles with honesty and build healthier, more fulfilling relationships.

Chapter 10

Celebrating Truthfulness and Personal Growth

Overcoming patterns of dishonesty and building healthier habits can be challenging and ongoing. It takes time, commitment, and a willingness to be vulnerable and open with oneself and others. However, individuals can create a positive and empowering environment for change by focusing on personal growth and celebrating moments of truthfulness.

One way to celebrate truthfulness and personal growth is to set achievable goals and milestones. This may involve setting specific targets for honesty, such as committing to telling the truth in a particular situation or sharing a complex reality with a loved one. Individuals can build momentum toward lasting change by setting achievable goals and celebrating each milestone.

It is also essential for individuals to acknowledge and celebrate moments of truthfulness and honesty, no matter how small. This may involve expressing gratitude and appreciation for a loved one's honesty or reflecting on personal growth and progress. By celebrating moments of honesty, individuals can reinforce positive behaviors and encourage themselves and others to strive toward truthfulness and personal development.

In addition to setting goals and celebrating moments of honesty, individuals must prioritize self-care and personal growth. This may involve engaging in activities that bring joy and fulfillment, practicing mindfulness and meditation, and seeking support from friends or a therapist. By prioritizing personal growth and self-care, individuals can improve their overall mental health and well-being, which can, in turn, support their ability to be truthful and honest with themselves and others.

It is also essential for individuals to be mindful of the language they use when discussing honesty and personal growth. Rather than focusing on shame or guilt for past behaviors, individuals should approach the process of personal development with a sense of curiosity, openness, and self-compassion. By reframing the conversation around personal growth and change, individuals can create a more positive and empowering environment for themselves and others.

Another way to celebrate truthfulness and personal growth is to express gratitude and appreciation for those who support individuals on their journey toward honesty and personal development. This may involve thanking loved ones for their patience and support or acknowledging the efforts of a therapist or counselor who has helped individuals work through patterns of dishonesty. By expressing gratitude and appreciation, individuals can reinforce positive behaviors and create a sense of community around personal growth and change.

It is also essential for individuals to be open and honest with themselves and others about their struggles with honesty and personal growth. This may involve acknowledging mistakes and setbacks and taking responsibility for past behaviors. By being honest and transparent, individuals can create a safe and supportive environment for personal growth and change.

Celebrating truthfulness and personal growth requires honesty, vulnerability, and self-compassion. By setting achievable goals, acknowledging and celebrating moments of honesty, prioritizing self-care and personal development, reframing the conversation around personal growth and change, expressing gratitude and appreciation, and being open and honest about struggles and setbacks, individuals can create a positive and empowering environment for personal growth and lasting change.

Overcoming patterns of dishonesty and building healthier habits is a challenging and ongoing process. However, by focusing on personal growth, celebrating moments of honesty, and creating a supportive and empowering environment, individuals can overcome patterns of dishonesty and build healthier, more fulfilling relationships. In addition, by committing to personal growth and change, individuals can create a more positive and honest future for themselves and those around them.

Another way to celebrate truthfulness and personal growth is to recognize the importance of forgiveness. It can be difficult for individuals to forgive themselves or others for past mistakes or patterns of dishonesty. However, forgiveness is essential to personal growth and can help individuals move forward with a sense of peace and closure.

Forgiveness involves acknowledging past mistakes and making amends while being compassionate and understanding towards oneself and others. Individuals need to recognize that forgiveness is a process that may take time to heal from past hurts or betrayals. However, individuals can create a more positive and supportive environment for personal growth and change by cultivating a sense of forgiveness and compassion.

It is also crucial for individuals to recognize that personal growth and change can be a source of inspiration and motivation for others. By openly discussing the process of personal growth and sharing successes and challenges with loved ones, individuals can inspire others to work towards honesty and personal growth in their own lives. This can create a sense of community and support around personal growth and change and help reinforce positive behaviors and attitudes toward honesty.

Additionally, celebrating truthfulness and personal growth can involve creating a supportive and empowering environment for oneself and others. This may include setting boundaries, communicating needs in relationships, or creating a safe and supportive space for others to share their struggles and successes. Individuals can reinforce positive behaviors and attitudes toward honesty and personal growth by creating a supportive and empowering environment. As a result, they can help to make lasting changes in their own lives and the lives of others.

Celebrating truthfulness and personal growth requires honesty, vulnerability, and self-compassion. By setting achievable goals, acknowledging and celebrating moments of honesty, prioritizing self-care and personal development, reframing the conversation around personal growth and change, expressing gratitude and appreciation, being open and honest about struggles and setbacks, recognizing the importance of forgiveness, inspiring and supporting others, and creating a supportive and empowering environment, individuals can make a positive and lasting impact on their own lives and the lives of those around them.

Book 3

Ending Abusive Behavior in Relationships

Chapter 1

Understanding Abuse

Abuse can take many forms and be challenging and complex to navigate. It can occur in any relationship, including romantic partnerships, family relationships, and friendships. Understanding abuse, its different forms, and its impact on individuals is an essential step in preventing and addressing abusive behavior.

A critical aspect of understanding abuse is recognizing its different forms. For example, physical abuse involves using force or violence to harm an individual. In contrast, emotional abuse involves behaviors that undermine an individual's self-esteem, emotional well-being, and sense of worth. Sexual abuse involves unwanted or coerced sexual contact or conduct, while financial abuse involves misusing or controlling an individual's financial resources.

It is also important to recognize abuse's impact on individuals. Abusive behavior can cause physical harm but also have long-lasting emotional and psychological effects. This may include feelings of shame, guilt, low self-worth, and symptoms of anxiety, depression, and post-traumatic stress disorder (PTSD). In severe cases, abuse can even lead to physical injury or death.

Another aspect of understanding abuse is recognizing the patterns and dynamics that can contribute to abusive behavior. This may involve examining societal and cultural factors perpetuating gender-based violence, power imbalances within relationships, and underlying psychological factors such as trauma, insecurity, and a need for control. By understanding the root causes of abusive behavior, individuals can work towards preventing and addressing abuse in all its forms.

It is also essential to recognize that abusive behavior is never the victim's fault. Abuse victims often experience shame, guilt, and self-blame, but it is necessary to understand that abusive behavior is always the perpetrator's responsibility. No one deserves to be abused; it is never the victim's fault.

Preventing and addressing abuse involves a collective effort from individuals, communities, and society. This may include promoting healthy relationship dynamics, such as open communication, mutual respect, and equality. It may also involve challenging harmful social norms and attitudes that perpetuate abusive behavior, such as accepting violence or normalizing controlling behaviors.

Addressing abusive behavior also involves providing support and resources for victims. This may include counseling, therapy, legal resources, and emergency shelter services. In addition, individuals and communities can work towards preventing and addressing abuse by providing a safe and supportive environment for victims.

It is also essential to hold perpetrators of abuse accountable for their behavior. This may involve reporting abuse to authorities, seeking legal action, or confronting perpetrators directly. Perpetrators need to be held responsible for their behavior, which conveys that abusive behavior will not be tolerated.

Finally, it is essential to recognize that healing from the effects of abuse can be a long and challenging process. This may involve seeking therapy or counseling, practicing self-care and self-compassion, and building a support network of trusted individuals. By prioritizing healing and self-care, abuse victims can work towards overcoming the effects of abusive behavior and rebuilding their sense of self-worth and well-being.

In addition to recognizing the different forms of abuse and its impact, it is essential to understand the warning signs of abusive behavior. These may include controlling behaviors such as isolation from friends and family, limiting access to financial resources, and monitoring phone and internet usage. Other warning signs may include verbal abuse, threats of violence, and physical aggression.

Trusting your instincts and taking action if you suspect someone you know is experiencing abusive behavior is essential. This may involve reaching out to the individual, offering support and resources, or reporting the behavior to authorities. It is necessary to approach the situation with sensitivity and understanding, as individuals experiencing abusive behavior may feel isolated and ashamed.

It is also essential to recognize that abusive behavior can occur in any relationship, regardless of age, gender, sexual orientation, or socioeconomic status. However, children, teenagers, and elderly individuals are particularly vulnerable to abuse, and it is essential to be aware of the warning signs and to take action if necessary.

For individuals experiencing abusive behavior, it is essential to know that resources and support are available. This may include seeking counseling or therapy, contacting a trusted friend or family member, or contacting a hotline or advocacy organization. In addition, it is essential to prioritize your safety and well-being and to take action to protect yourself from further harm.

In conclusion, understanding abuse is essential in preventing and addressing abusive behavior. This involves recognizing the different forms of abuse, understanding the warning signs, and taking action to promote healthy relationship dynamics and provide support and resources for victims. By working towards preventing and addressing abusive behavior, individuals and communities can create a safer, more supportive, and more equitable world for all.

Chapter 2

Cultivating Healthy Relationship Skills

Healthy relationships are a cornerstone of a fulfilling life. However, cultivating and maintaining healthy relationships takes effort and skill. This chapter will explore the critical skills necessary for developing healthy relationships, including effective Communication, empathy, trust, and boundary setting.

Effective Communication is the foundation of any healthy relationship. Communication involves both expressing oneself honestly and listening actively to others. This means being clear and direct in expressing one's needs and feelings and also being receptive to the needs and feelings of others. In addition, effective Communication requires empathy, respect, and a willingness to work toward mutual understanding.

Empathy is the ability to understand and share the feelings of others. Empathy is a critical component of healthy relationships, as it allows individuals to connect on a deeper level and support each other through difficult times. Cultivating empathy involves actively listening to others, acknowledging their feelings, and validating their experiences. This can include reflecting on what you have heard, expressing empathy and understanding, and offering support and encouragement.

Trust is another essential component of healthy relationships. Trust involves feeling safe and secure with another person and being able to rely on them for emotional support and guidance. Building trust requires honesty, reliability, and consistency in words and actions. Trust is built over time through open Communication, transparency, and a commitment to maintaining healthy relationships.

Boundary Setting Healthy relationships also requires clear and compelling boundary setting. Limitations involve limiting what is and is not acceptable behavior in a relationship. This can include setting physical, emotional, and social boundaries and communicating these boundaries clearly to others. Setting and enforcing limits requires assertiveness, self-respect, and a willingness to prioritize one's needs and well-being.

Cultivating healthy relationship skills is a lifelong process that requires ongoing effort and practice. The following tips may be helpful for individuals seeking to improve their relationship skills:

1. Practice active listening. This involves listening attentively to others, reflecting on what you have heard, and expressing empathy and understanding.

2. Communicate openly and honestly. This means being clear and direct in expressing your needs and feelings and being receptive to the needs and feelings of others. It also means being willing to have difficult conversations when necessary and being open to feedback and constructive criticism.

3. Build trust through consistency and reliability. This involves honesty and character in your words and actions and following through on your commitments. It also means being willing to be vulnerable and share your own experiences and feelings with others.

4. Set clear boundaries and communicate them assertively. This means sharing your limits clearly and directly and enforcing them when necessary. It also means respecting the boundaries of others and being willing to negotiate and compromise when necessary.

5. Seek support and guidance when needed. This may involve seeking counseling or therapy or contacting trusted friends or family members for support. It also means being willing to ask for help when you need it and offering support and guidance to others when they need it.

Cultivating healthy relationship skills is essential to building and maintaining fulfilling relationships. This involves effective Communication, empathy, trust, and boundary setting. By prioritizing these skills and committing to ongoing growth and development, individuals can create healthier, more supportive, and more fulfilling relationships in all areas of life. It is important to remember that healthy relationships require effort and ongoing attention, but the rewards are well worth the investment.

Continuing from the tips mentioned earlier, it's also important to practice self-awareness regarding your own behavior in relationships. This involves taking an honest look at your actions and thought patterns and being willing to identify and address any areas for growth or improvement.

For example, find yourself consistently struggling with trust issues in relationships. Exploring the root causes of these issues and working on developing greater emotional resilience and self-confidence may be helpful. Alternatively, suppose you are overly critical or judgmental towards others. In that case, it may be beneficial to cultivate greater compassion and empathy for others and to work on developing a more positive and supportive mindset.

Another important aspect of cultivating healthy relationship skills is being willing to compromise and work through conflicts constructively and respectfully. This involves being willing to listen to the perspectives of others, to acknowledge and validate their feelings, and to work towards finding mutually beneficial solutions to problems.

Sometimes, seeking outside support or guidance may be necessary to work through more challenging conflicts or relationship issues. This may involve seeking counseling or therapy or engaging in couples or family therapy sessions to work through more complex dynamics.

Cultivating healthy relationship skills requires ongoing effort, self-reflection, and a commitment to growth and development. By prioritizing effective Communication, empathy, trust, and boundary setting, individuals can build healthier, more fulfilling relationships in all areas of life. With time and practice, these skills can become second nature, and individuals can enjoy the many benefits of healthy and supportive relationships.

Chapter 3

Establishing Accountability and Boundaries

Establishing boundaries and accountability is an essential aspect of building healthy relationships. Boundaries are the physical, emotional, and mental limits that people set for themselves to protect their well-being and ensure their needs are met. Accountability, on the other hand, refers to the responsibility that individuals take for their actions and the consequences that come with them. By establishing clear boundaries and being accountable for their actions, individuals can cultivate healthier, more respectful relationships with others.

Boundaries can take many forms and can be different for each individual. However, some common types of limitations include:

1. Physical boundaries refer to the space around an individual's body and can include boundaries around touch, personal area, and physical activities.

2. Emotional boundaries: Emotional boundaries refer to the limits around an individual's vibrant energy and capacity and can include setting boundaries around topics of conversation, expressing emotions, and being vulnerable.

3. Mental boundaries: Mental boundaries refer to the limits around an individual's thoughts and beliefs, and can include limitations around what information is shared, what topics are discussed, and what opinions are expressed.

4. Time boundaries: Time boundaries refer to the limits around an individual's time and schedule and can include boundaries around work hours, social commitments, and personal time.

When establishing boundaries, it's important to communicate them clearly and assertively while respecting others' needs and limitations. This can involve setting limits around specific behaviors or actions and being willing to enforce consequences if those boundaries are violated.

Accountability is also a crucial aspect of building healthy relationships. This involves taking responsibility for one's actions and acknowledging the impact that those actions have on others. When individuals are accountable for their behavior, they are more likely to address and change harmful patterns and work towards rebuilding trust and respect in relationships.

A critical tool for promoting relationship accountability is using "I" statements. This involves taking ownership of one's feelings and actions and communicating them in a clear and non-blaming way. For example, instead of saying, "You always do this to me," an individual might say, "I feel hurt when this happens."

Another critical aspect of accountability is being willing to apologize when necessary. This involves acknowledging any harm that has been caused, expressing remorse, and making a commitment to change going forward. Apologizing can be difficult, but it is essential to rebuilding trust and respect in relationships.

Establishing boundaries and accountability is particularly important in situations with a history of abuse or trauma. In these cases, setting clear boundaries can help to protect individuals from further harm. In contrast, accountability can help to ensure that the perpetrator takes responsibility for their actions and works towards change.

It's also important to recognize that boundaries and accountability are not just about setting limits and consequences. They are also about promoting positive behaviors and communication in relationships. By setting clear expectations and communicating respectfully and honestly, individuals can cultivate healthier, more supportive relationships with those around them.

Some strategies for promoting healthy boundaries and accountability in relationships include:

1. Communicate openly and honestly: Be willing to express your needs and expectations clearly, and

to listen to the perspectives of others without judgment or defensiveness.

2. Practice active listening: Try hearing and understanding what others say honestly and responding thoughtfully and respectfully.

3. Use "I" statements: Take ownership of your feelings and actions, and communicate them in a non-blaming way.

4. Set clear boundaries: Be willing to assertively communicate your limits and expectations and enforce consequences if those boundaries are violated.

5. Be accountable for your actions: Take responsibility for your behavior, and be willing to acknowledge and address any harm that has been caused

6. Apologize when necessary: Be willing to acknowledge any harm caused, express remorse, and commit to change going forward.

7. Seek professional help: If you are struggling with establishing boundaries or being accountable for your behavior, seeking support from a therapist or counselor may be helpful.

8. Practice self-care: Taking care of your physical, emotional, and mental health can help you better establish and maintain healthy boundaries and be more accountable for your behavior.

It's important to note that establishing boundaries and promoting accountability is not a one-time task but rather an ongoing process. As individuals grow and change, their limitations and expectations may shift, and it's important to continue communicating and adjusting accordingly.

One typical challenge individuals face regarding boundaries and accountability is navigating power dynamics in relationships. This can be particularly challenging in situations with a significant power imbalance, such as in cases of domestic abuse or workplace harassment.
In these situations, seeking outside support and resources, such as counseling or legal assistance, is essential. It may also be helpful to reach out to trusted friends or family members for help and develop a safety plan for responding to potentially dangerous situations.

Establishing healthy boundaries and promoting accountability in relationships requires a willingness to be honest, communicate openly, and take responsibility for one's behavior. By doing so, individuals can cultivate respectful, supportive, and fulfilling relationships for all involved.

Chapter 4

Unraveling the Roots of Abusive Behavior

Abusive behavior is a complex issue that can significantly impact individuals, families, and communities. While many factors can contribute to abusive behavior, it's often rooted in personal and societal factors.

One of the critical factors that can contribute to abusive behavior is a history of trauma or abuse. In addition, individuals who have experienced trauma or abuse may be more likely to engage in abusive behavior, as they may struggle with feelings of powerlessness or low self-esteem.

In addition, abusive behavior can be fueled by a range of emotions, such as anger, jealousy, or insecurity. These emotions can be challenging to manage, particularly if individuals lack the skills or support to navigate them healthily.

Another factor that can contribute to abusive behavior is socialization. In many societies, traditional gender roles can reinforce beliefs about power and control in relationships, leading to abusive behavior. Additionally, individuals who grow up in households where abusive behavior is present may be more likely to perpetuate these patterns in their relationships.

Understanding the roots of abusive behavior is essential in addressing and preventing it. This often involves a combination of self-reflection, education, and seeking support from trained professionals.

Some key strategies for unraveling the roots of abusive behavior include:

1. Acknowledging the problem: The first step in addressing abusive behavior is admitting it exists. This can be a difficult and uncomfortable process, but it's an essential first step towards healing and growth.

2. Seeking professional help: If you are struggling with abusive behavior, seeking support from a therapist or counselor may be helpful. A trained professional can help you understand your behavior's root causes better and develop strategies for managing difficult emotions and building healthy relationships.

3. Practicing self-reflection: Reflecting on your own experiences and beliefs can be a powerful way to understand the roots of abusive behavior better. Consider journaling, meditating, or speaking with a trusted friend or family member about your experiences.

4. Challenging societal norms: Recognizing that societal norms and expectations often reinforce abusive behavior is essential. By challenging these norms and working to promote healthier attitudes and behaviors, we can create a more just and equitable society for all.

5. Learning healthy relationship skills: Building healthy relationships requires a range of skills, including effective communication, conflict resolution, and empathy. Individuals can build more fulfilling and respectful relationships by learning and practicing these skills.

6. Practicing self-care: Managing difficult emotions and behaviors can be exhausting, and prioritizing self-care is essential. This can include engaging in activities that bring you joy, seeking support from friends and loved ones, or engaging in mindfulness practices like yoga or meditation.

7. Addressing underlying issues: Abusive behavior is often a symptom of underlying problems, such as trauma, addiction, or mental health challenges. By addressing these underlying issues, individuals can work through the root causes of their behavior and build healthier relationships.

8. Learning from past experiences: Past experiences of abusive behavior can be painful and difficult to process, but they can also provide valuable insights into the root causes of abusive behavior. By reflecting on past experiences and learning from them, individuals can gain a deeper understanding of their behavior and begin to make positive changes.

9. Taking responsibility: Individuals must take responsibility for their behavior and its impact on others. This may involve making amends, seeking forgiveness, or taking concrete steps to change one's behavior.

10. Building a support network: Overcoming abusive behavior can be a challenging process, and it's essential to have a strong support network in place. This may include friends, family members, therapists, or support groups.

It's important to note that unraveling the roots of abusive behavior is not a one-time task but an ongoing process. It requires a willingness, to be honest, reflective, and committed to growth and change. By doing so, individuals can break free from abusive behavior patterns and build healthier, more fulfilling relationships with themselves and others.

Ultimately, unraveling the roots of abusive behavior is a complex and ongoing process that requires a willingness, to be honest, reflective, and committed to growth and change. By addressing the underlying causes of abusive behavior, individuals can build healthier, more fulfilling relationships with themselves and others.

Chapter 5

Trauma, Abuse, and Healing

Trauma and abuse can profoundly impact a person's life, leaving deep emotional scars that can last for years. The effects of trauma and abuse can be especially devastating when it occurs in close relationships, such as romantic partnerships or familial relationships.

Individuals who have experienced trauma or abuse may develop maladaptive coping mechanisms, such as self-harm, substance abuse, or dissociation, to manage the overwhelming feelings and memories associated with their experiences. Unfortunately, these coping mechanisms may provide temporary relief but ultimately interfere with a person's ability to heal and move forward.

Fortunately, healing from trauma and abuse is possible. However, it is a process that takes time, patience, and a willingness to engage in self-reflection and self-care. Here are some critical steps toward healing:

1. Acknowledge the trauma and abuse: It can be challenging to confront the reality of trauma and abuse, but acknowledging the experiences is the first step towards healing. It's important to understand that the trauma and abuse were not your fault and that you deserve support and compassion.

2. Please seek professional help: Trauma and abuse can have complex effects on a person's mental health, and it's essential to seek professional help from a trained therapist or counselor. A therapist can help you work through your feelings, develop coping strategies, and process the trauma and abuse.

3. Practice self-care: Taking care of yourself is a vital part of the healing process. This can involve engaging in activities you enjoy, such as exercise or hobbies, practicing relaxation techniques like meditation or deep breathing, and prioritizing rest and sleep.

4. Build a support system: Healing from trauma and abuse can be a difficult journey, and having a supportive network of friends, family, and professionals can make a big difference. It's essential to surround yourself with people who uplift and support you and who can provide a safe and non-judgmental space for you to share your experiences.

5. Engage in trauma-focused therapies: Several evidence-based treatments can be effective in treating trauma and abuse, such as cognitive-behavioral therapy (CBT), eye movement desensitization and reprocessing (EMDR), and trauma-focused cognitive treatment (TF-CBT). These therapies can help you process and cope with traumatic memories and develop skills for managing distressing emotions and thoughts.

6. Practice self-compassion: It's essential to treat yourself with kindness and compassion as you navigate the healing process. This can involve offering yourself encouragement, recognizing your strengths and resilience, and allowing yourself to experience a range of emotions without judgment.

7. Set boundaries: If you are currently in a relationship with someone who has caused trauma or abuse, setting boundaries or even ending the relationship may be necessary to prioritize your safety and well-being. It's essential to communicate your boundaries clearly and assertively and to seek support from loved ones and professionals if necessary.

It's important to note that healing from trauma and abuse is not linear. It may involve setbacks and relapses, and it's common to experience difficult emotions such as anger, fear, and sadness. However, with time and support, these difficult emotions can be processed and integrated into a larger narrative of growth and healing. It's also important to recognize that healing from trauma and abuse is not solely an individual process but a collective one. It requires a shift in societal attitudes towards trauma and abuse and a willingness to prioritize the safety and well-being of survivors. This can involve advocating for policies that support survivors, such as increased funding for mental health services and trauma-informed care and challenging harmful beliefs and stereotypes about survivors.

Healing from trauma and abuse is a challenging and complex journey, but it is a journey that is worth taking. With time, support, and a commitment to self-growth, survivors can find healing and build lives of joy and fulfillment.

Healing from trauma and abuse is a process that requires time, patience, and a willingness to engage in self-reflection and self-care. You can move towards a life of healing and growth by acknowledging your experiences, seeking professional help, practicing self-care, building a support system, engaging in trauma-focused therapies, practicing self-compassion, and setting boundaries. Remember that you deserve love, support, and healing and that it's never too late to start the journey toward a brighter future.

Chapter 6

Building Emotional Resilience

Emotional resilience is the ability to adapt and recover from stress and adversity. It's a critical aspect of mental health that enables individuals to cope with life's challenges and maintain their emotional well-being. Building emotional resilience is an ongoing process that requires intention, effort, and practice. In this chapter, we'll explore some key strategies to help you build emotional resilience and thrive in adversity.

1. Cultivate Positive Emotions Cultivating positive emotions is essential to building emotional resilience. Positive emotions like joy, gratitude, love, and contentment can help counteract negative emotions like stress, anxiety, and depression. Engage in activities that bring you joy, such as spending time with loved ones, pursuing hobbies, or engaging in physical exercise. Make a conscious effort to focus on the

positive aspects of your life and practice gratitude regularly.

2. Practice Mindfulness Mindfulness is being present at the moment, without judgment. It can help reduce stress, improve mood, and increase emotional resilience. Mindfulness can be practiced through meditation, yoga, or other relaxation techniques. Make it a habit to incorporate mindfulness into your daily routine, even just for a few minutes.

3. Build a Support Network A strong support network is crucial for building emotional resilience. Surround yourself with people who uplift and support you. Make time for friends and family, and participate in social activities that bring you joy. If you're struggling with emotional difficulties, consider joining a support group or seeking professional help.

4. Practice Self-Care Self-care is taking care of your physical, emotional, and mental health. It includes getting enough sleep, eating a balanced diet, exercising regularly, and engaging in activities that bring you joy. Prioritize self-care in your daily routine, and care for yourself intentionally.

5. Develop Coping Skills Developing coping skills is crucial to building emotional resilience. Coping skills can help you manage stress and difficult emotions effectively. Examples of coping skills include deep breathing, journaling, positive self-talk, and relaxation techniques.

Identify coping skills that work for you and practice them regularly.

6. Embrace a Growth Mindset A growth mindset is the belief that one's abilities and qualities can be developed through dedication and hard work. Embracing a growth mindset can help build emotional resilience by enabling you to view challenges as opportunities for growth. Focus on progress rather than perfection and be open to learning from mistakes and failures.

7. Seek Professional Help When Necessary If you're struggling with emotional difficulties, don't hesitate to seek professional help. Mental health professionals can provide support, guidance, and evidence-based interventions to help you build emotional resilience and improve overall well-being.

To build emotional resilience, learning how to cope with negative emotions is essential. One way to do this is through practicing self-care. Self-care involves engaging in activities that promote physical, emotional, and mental well-being. This includes exercise, meditation, time in nature, journaling, and socializing with loved ones.

Another way to build emotional resilience is to develop healthy coping mechanisms for managing stress. This can include techniques such as deep breathing, mindfulness, and positive self-talk. Learning how to set healthy boundaries and say no to requests or activities not aligned with your values or priorities is also essential.

Additionally, building emotional resilience requires a willingness to seek support from others. This can involve contacting friends, family members, or a therapist. Talking about your emotions with a trusted individual can provide relief and support.

It is also essential to cultivate a growth mindset. This involves viewing challenges as opportunities for growth and learning rather than insurmountable obstacles. It consists of developing a sense of self-efficacy, or the belief that you can handle difficult situations and overcome adversity.

Furthermore, building emotional resilience involves practicing self-compassion. This means treating yourself with kindness and understanding rather than harshly criticizing yourself for perceived shortcomings or mistakes. It consists of acknowledging and accepting difficult emotions, being gentle with yourself, and recognizing your strengths.

Building emotional resilience is an ongoing process that requires a commitment to self-care, healthy coping mechanisms, seeking support, cultivating a growth mindset, and practicing self-compassion. By developing these skills, individuals can enhance their ability to cope with challenges and adversity and maintain a sense of emotional well-being.

Chapter 7

Healthy Ways to Express Needs and Desires

Expressing our needs and desires is a crucial aspect of any healthy relationship. It allows for open communication, mutual respect, and understanding. However, expressing ourselves in an unhealthy way can lead to conflict, misunderstandings, and even resentment. Therefore, learning safe and healthy ways to express our needs and desires is essential, whether in our romantic relationships, friendships, or professional life.

One essential step in healthily expressing our needs and desires is identifying them. Take some time to reflect on what you truly need and want in your relationships. It can be helpful to list these needs and desires and prioritize them according to their importance.

Once you have identified your needs and desires, expressing them clearly and assertively is essential. This means stating what you need or want directly and respectfully. Avoid using passive-aggressive or manipulative language, which can cause confusion and conflict.

It's also important to be open to hearing and respecting the needs and desires of others. Healthy communication is a two-way street, and listening actively to others and acknowledging their needs and wishes is important. This helps to create a mutual sense of respect and understanding in the relationship.

Another critical aspect of healthily expressing our needs and desires is to be mindful of our tone and body language. Avoid using a confrontational or aggressive style; instead, aim for a calm and respectful one. Your body language can also communicate much, so be mindful of your facial expressions and gestures. In addition, it's essential to express our needs and desires at an appropriate time and place. Choose a time when both parties are calm and open to discussing the issue. Avoid bringing up sensitive topics when one or both parties feel stressed, tired, or distracted.

Furthermore, it's essential to be open to compromise and negotiation. Healthy communication involves finding a middle ground where both parties needs and desires can be met. This means being willing to listen and make concessions to reach a mutually beneficial outcome.

In some cases, it may be helpful to seek the assistance of a professional, such as a therapist or mediator, to facilitate healthy communication and problem-solving in the relationship.

Overall, expressing our needs and desires safely and healthily is essential for creating and maintaining healthy relationships. By being transparent, assertive, respectful, mindful, and open to compromise and negotiation, we can build stronger and more fulfilling connections with those around us.

Another vital aspect of healthily expressing our needs and desires is avoiding making assumptions or mind-reading. It's essential to communicate clearly and directly rather than assuming the other person knows what you need or want. Similarly, avoid believing that you know what the other person is thinking or feeling. Instead, ask for clarification and encourage open and honest communication.

It's also important to be aware of any barriers to communication, such as cultural differences or past experiences. These barriers can affect how we express ourselves and interpret the messages of others. Being mindful of these barriers and working to overcome them can facilitate healthy communication and understanding.

Furthermore, it's important to recognize the difference between needs and wants. Needs are essential to our well-being and survival, while wants are desires that may be nice to have but are not essential. Therefore, it's important to prioritize our needs over our wants and communicate them clearly to others.

In addition, it's important to practice self-care and self-compassion when expressing our needs and desires. This means acknowledging our own emotions and needs and communicating them in a way that is respectful and kind. It also means being open to hearing feedback and criticism in a non-defensive form and using it as an opportunity for growth and self-improvement.

Chapter 8

Seeking Professional Help for Abusive Behavior

Seeking professional help is a vital step in addressing and overcoming abusive behavior. Whether you have been the perpetrator of abuse or the victim, seeking help from a trained professional can aid in the healing and recovery process.

When seeking professional help for abusive behavior, it is vital to find a therapist or counselor with experience dealing with this issue. A good therapist should provide a non-judgmental and safe environment to discuss your thoughts and feelings. They should also help you identify the underlying causes of your abusive behavior and provide strategies to overcome it.

Various types of therapy can be beneficial for addressing abusive behavior. Cognitive-behavioral therapy (CBT) is one approach that focuses on identifying and changing negative thought patterns and behaviors that contribute to abuse. Another therapy that may be effective is dialectical behavior therapy (DBT), which helps individuals regulate their emotions and develop healthy coping mechanisms.

Group therapy can also be a helpful form of support for those struggling with abusive behavior. Group therapy provides a safe environment for individuals to share their experiences and connect with others who have similar struggles. It also offers the opportunity to receive others' feedback, support, and accountability.

In addition to therapy, there are other steps you can take to address abusive behavior. First, it is essential to take responsibility for your actions and make a commitment to change. This may involve apologizing to those you have harmed, setting boundaries for yourself, and repairing damaged relationships.

Recognizing and addressing any underlying mental health issues contributing to your abusive behavior is also essential. This may involve seeking treatment for depression, anxiety, or other mental health disorders.

When seeking professional help for abusive behavior, being open and honest with your therapist or counselor is essential. This includes being willing to discuss complex and uncomfortable topics and being receptive to feedback and constructive criticism. It is also important to remain committed to the change process and be patient with yourself as you work toward healing and recovery.

In addition to seeking professional help, various resources are available to those struggling with abusive behavior. Support groups, helplines, and online forums can provide a safe and confidential space for individuals to seek support and advice.

It is important to note that seeking professional help for abusive behavior is not a sign of weakness or failure. Instead, it is a courageous step towards healing and creating positive change in your life. A trained professional can help you develop the tools and skills to overcome abusive behavior and build healthy relationships.

Overall, seeking professional help for abusive behavior is vital to healing and recovery. Finding a therapist or counselor who specializes in addressing abusive behavior and remains committed to the change process is essential. Remember, healing and recovery are possible with the proper support and resources. The road to recovery from abusive behavior is long and challenging, and seeking professional help is essential in this journey. Unfortunately, it's not easy to confront one's harmful behavior and patterns, and it takes a great deal of courage to admit that you need help.

A qualified therapist or counselor can help you understand the underlying causes of your abusive behavior and develop strategies to manage it. They can also help you explore any underlying mental health issues contributing to your behavior, such as anxiety, depression, or trauma.

In addition to individual therapy, group therapy can be valuable for those struggling with abusive behavior. Group therapy provides a safe and supportive space for individuals to share their experiences and learn from others who are going through similar struggles. Various specialized programs and resources are also available for those seeking help with abusive behavior. These may include anger management programs, domestic violence support groups, and other community resources.

It's important to note that seeking professional help for abusive behavior does not mean you are weak or flawed. It takes immense strength and courage to confront your harmful behavior and take steps to change it.

If you are struggling with abusive behavior, it's important to remember that you are not alone and that help is available. By seeking professional service and support, you can begin to heal and build healthier, more fulfilling relationships with those around you.

Seeking professional help for abusive behavior is crucial in healing and recovery. A qualified therapist or counselor can help you understand the underlying causes of your behavior and develop strategies to manage it. Group therapy and specialized programs can also be valuable resources. Remember that seeking help is a sign of strength and that there is hope for a better future.

Chapter 9

Supporting Loved Ones in Healing from Abuse

Abuse can leave deep emotional scars that require time and patience to heal. While survivors of abuse may have different healing journeys, having the support of loved ones can be an essential part of the process. Here are some ways to support loved ones in healing from abuse.

First and foremost, listen without judgment. Survivors of abuse may feel shame, fear, and self-doubt, and it is essential to create a safe space for them to share their thoughts and feelings. It is crucial not to force them to speak if they feel uncomfortable, as this can cause them to withdraw further. Let them know that you believe them and that they do not deserve to be abused.

Another way to support loved ones is to help them create a safety plan. This plan can include practical steps if the abuser contacts or tries to harm them again. Please encourage them to document any incidents of abuse, including texts, emails, or calls, and keep them in a safe place. If the situation is severe, consider contacting law enforcement or a domestic violence hotline for additional support.

Encourage self-care and self-compassion. Survivors of abuse may have internalized negative messages about themselves, so it is crucial to remind them that they are worthy of love and respect. In addition, please encourage them to take care of themselves physically and emotionally, such as engaging in activities they enjoy, getting enough sleep, and practicing relaxation techniques like yoga or meditation.

Be patient and understanding. Healing from abuse is a long process; survivors may experience setbacks or triggers that remind them of their trauma. Being patient and avoiding pressuring them to move on or get over it quickly is essential. Let them know that you are there to support them through their healing journey, no matter how long it takes.

Please encourage them to seek professional help. Healing from abuse often requires the use of a professional therapist or counselor. Encourage your loved ones to seek out a qualified mental health professional with experience working with abuse survivors. If they are not ready to seek help, let them know that it is okay and that you will be there for them when they are ready.

Respect their boundaries. Survivors of abuse may have difficulty trusting others or feeling safe around them. It is crucial to respect their boundaries and not push them to do anything they are not ready for. If they need space or time, respect their wishes and tell them you will be there when they are ready.

Please educate yourself on abuse and its effects. Learning about abuse and its impact can help you understand what your loved one is going through and how you can best support them. Many resources are available, including books, articles, and support groups.

You can also offer emotional support by being present and available to them. Let them know you are there to listen and offer a shoulder to cry on. Encourage them to seek professional help, such as therapy or counseling, and contribute to helping them find resources if needed.

It is also essential to respect your loved one's boundaries and needs. For example, avoid pushing them to talk about things they may not be ready to share, and respect their decisions about what kind of help they want and when they want it.

In addition to emotional support, you can also offer practical support. This may include helping them with daily tasks, providing a safe place to stay, or helping them navigate legal or financial issues related to the abuse.

It is important to remember that healing from abuse is long and arduous, and there may be setbacks and challenges. Be patient and understanding, and continue to offer your support and encouragement even when things are tough.

Finally, take care of yourself as well. Supporting a loved one through healing from abuse can be emotionally taxing, so it is essential to prioritize your self-care and seek support for yourself as needed.

Supporting a loved one through healing from abuse is challenging but essential. By offering emotional and practical support, respecting their boundaries and needs, and caring for themselves, you can help your loved one on their journey toward healing and recovery. Remember to be patient, understanding, and compassionate, and always believe in your loved one's strength and resilience.

Chapter 10

Fostering Forgiveness and Reconciliation

Forgiveness is a powerful tool in healing emotional wounds and finding closure from past traumas. When it comes to abusive behavior in relationships, forgiving the abuser can be complicated. However, forgiveness can also lead to reconciliation and growth for both parties. Here are some ways to foster forgiveness and reconciliation in the aftermath of abuse.

First and foremost, it's essential to acknowledge and validate your emotions. Forgiving someone doesn't mean you must forget or downplay the hurt they caused you. It's okay to feel angry, hurt, and betrayed. Allow yourself to feel these emotions and healthily work through them.

Once you've acknowledged your emotions, consider the possibility of forgiveness. This doesn't mean that you have to forgive the abuser automatically, but rather that you're open to forgiveness in the future. Forgiveness is a process, and it takes time to work through.

To foster forgiveness, creating a safe and supportive environment is essential. This could include seeking therapy, joining a support group, or confiding in trusted friends and family members. Surrounding yourself with positivity and support can help you work through your emotions and find the strength to forgive.

When you're ready, consider reaching out to the abuser. This could be in the form of a letter, phone call, or in-person meeting. But, again, it's essential to set boundaries and clarify that the communication's purpose is to work toward forgiveness and reconciliation rather than to rekindle the relationship.

During the conversation, it's essential to express your feelings and needs in a straightforward and non-confrontational way. It's also important to listen to the abuser's perspective and validate their emotions. This doesn't mean you have to excuse or condone their behavior, but rather that you're willing to hear them out and work towards understanding.

Both parties must be committed to making changes and rebuilding trust to move toward reconciliation. This could include seeking couples therapy, working on individual treatment, or creating a plan for accountability and growth. It's essential to have open and honest communication throughout this process and to hold each other accountable for any setbacks or mistakes.

Forgiveness and reconciliation are not easy processes, especially in cases of abuse. It's essential to prioritize your safety and well-being throughout the process and seek professional help. Remember that forgiveness is a personal decision and doesn't necessarily mean you must maintain a relationship with the abuser. Sometimes, forgiveness can be a tool for closure and personal growth rather than reconciliation.

When seeking forgiveness and reconciliation, it is essential to acknowledge the harm that was caused and take responsibility for it. This means genuinely apologizing for the actions that led to the hurt and demonstrating a commitment to making things right through words and actions.

In some cases, it may be necessary to seek the guidance of a professional therapist or mediator to facilitate the process of forgiveness and reconciliation. This can be especially helpful in situations where communication has broken down or where there is a lot of tension and conflict.

Forgiveness and reconciliation can be complex, and it may take time to rebuild trust and repair damaged relationships. Therefore, being patient and communicating openly and honestly throughout the process is essential. It may also be helpful to set realistic expectations and boundaries and to focus on the present rather than dwelling on past mistakes or hurts.

It is important to note that forgiveness does not mean condoning or excusing harmful behavior. Instead, it is a way to move forward and find peace after experiencing hurt and pain. It is also important to prioritize one's safety and well-being and seek professional help if necessary to ensure that abusive behavior does not continue.

In conclusion, fostering forgiveness and reconciliation is vital to personal growth and healthy relationships. It requires taking responsibility for harmful actions, demonstrating a commitment to making things right, prioritizing open communication, and a willingness to listen and understand. With patience, understanding, and a desire to work together, repairing damaged relationships and moving toward a happier, healthier future is possible.

Book 4

Detoxifying One's Personality

Chapter 1

Identifying Toxic Traits

Toxic traits can have a detrimental impact on individuals and their relationships with others. Therefore, recognizing these traits in oneself is crucial in addressing them and promoting personal growth. Here are some common toxic characteristics to be aware of:

1. Narcissism - A tendency to be self-centered and focused on personal gain at the expense of others.

2. Jealousy and Envy - A tendency to become resentful and bitter towards others for their successes, possessions, or achievements.

3. Controlling Behavior - A desire to manipulate or dominate others to feel powerful or in control.

4. Anger and Aggression - A tendency to lash out or become violent towards others, often in response to stress or frustration.

5. Blaming and Shaming - A tendency to shift responsibility onto others and use shame to maintain control or avoid accountability.

6. Dishonesty and Deception - A tendency to lie or manipulate to avoid consequences or gain an advantage.

7. Lack of Empathy - A difficulty understanding or acknowledging the feelings and perspectives of others.

Identifying these toxic traits in oneself can be difficult, as they often arise out of deeply ingrained patterns of thought and behavior. However, acknowledging their presence is the first step in addressing them and working towards personal growth.

It is important to note that having a toxic trait does not make someone a "bad person." Instead, it reflects areas in which one may need to focus their attention and work towards improvement.

If you struggle to identify toxic traits in yourself, seeking the input of trusted friends or family members can be helpful. In addition, they can provide valuable insight into areas where you could benefit from personal growth.

Additionally, seeking the help of a mental health professional can be a powerful tool in identifying and addressing toxic traits. A therapist or counselor can provide a safe space to explore these patterns and work towards healthier thinking and behavior.

By identifying toxic traits and working towards personal growth, individuals can cultivate more positive relationships with others and live happier, healthier lives.

Once you have identified your toxic traits, the next step is to work on changing them. This requires self-reflection, self-awareness, and a commitment to personal growth. Here are some strategies to help you in this process:

1. Acceptance - Acknowledge that you have toxic traits that need to be addressed. Denying or minimizing the problem will only prolong your suffering and cause harm to yourself and others. Embrace the fact that change is possible and commit to self-improvement.

2. Self-reflection - Reflect on your thoughts, feelings, and actions. What triggers your toxic behavior? What emotions are you trying to avoid or cope with? Journaling or talking to a therapist can help you gain deeper insights into your patterns and behaviors.

3. Education - Read books, attend workshops, or seek professional guidance to learn more about your toxic traits. This will help you better understand the root causes of your behavior and provide you with the knowledge and tools to make positive changes.

4. Self-compassion - Be kind to yourself during this process. Changing toxic behavior takes time and effort, and setbacks are inevitable. Remember that you are not defined by your harmful traits and that self-compassion can help you stay motivated and focused on your goals.

5. Accountability - Hold yourself accountable for your actions and behavior. This means taking

responsibility for the harm you have caused and making amends where possible. It also means being honest with yourself and others about your progress and setbacks.

6. Support - Surround yourself with people who support your journey towards positive change. This can include friends, family, or a therapist who can offer guidance and encouragement. Joining a support group or online community can also provide you with the necessary resources and motivation to stay on track.

7. Practice-Changing toxic behavior takes practice and repetition. Start by identifying one harmful trait you want to change and focus on until you see progress. Celebrate your successes along the way and stay committed to self-improvement.

Remember, identifying and changing toxic traits is a lifelong journey. It requires patience, self-awareness, and a willingness to learn and grow. However, with the right mindset and tools, it is possible to overcome toxic behavior and create a more positive and fulfilling life.

Chapter 2

Developing Emotional Intelligence

Emotional intelligence is crucial in building healthy relationships and promoting personal growth. Emotional intelligence involves the ability to understand and manage one's emotions, as well as the feelings of others. It is a skill that can be developed and honed over time through self-reflection, practice, and seeking feedback from others. In this chapter, we will explore the importance of emotional intelligence and strategies for developing it.

Emotional intelligence is essential for building healthy relationships and fostering personal growth. It helps us understand our emotions and how they impact our behavior and relationships with others. Emotional intelligence allows us to empathize, understand their feelings, and respond appropriately. It is an essential skill in navigating social situations and maintaining positive relationships.

In addition, emotional intelligence is linked to many positive outcomes, such as increased job performance, better mental health, and higher levels of life satisfaction. Those with high emotional intelligence are better equipped to handle stress, resolve conflicts, and communicate effectively. They are also more likely to be resilient in the face of adversity and have a greater sense of purpose and direction in life.

Strategies for Developing Emotional Intelligence Developing emotional intelligence takes time and effort, but it is a skill that can be learned and improved upon. Here are some strategies to help you build your emotional intelligence:

1. Practice Self-Awareness: Self-awareness is the foundation of emotional intelligence. Take time to reflect on your emotions, thoughts, and behaviors. Pay attention to how you feel in different situations and how you respond to those feelings.

2. Practice Mindfulness: Mindfulness involves being present at the moment and paying attention to your thoughts, feelings, and sensations without judgment. It can help you become more aware of your emotions and better understand how they impact your behavior.

3. Practice Empathy: Empathy is the ability to understand and share the feelings of others. Practice putting yourself in other people's shoes and try to understand their perspective. Listen actively and validate their feelings.

4. Practice Effective Communication: Effective communication is essential for building positive

relationships. Practice active listening, expressing your feelings clearly and respectfully, and being open to feedback.

5. Practice Self-Regulation: Self-regulation involves managing your emotions and behavior in response to different situations. Practice techniques such as deep breathing, visualization, and positive self-talk to help you regulate your emotions.

6. Seek Feedback: Ask for feedback from others on how you come across different situations. This can help you identify areas for improvement and develop a greater understanding of how your emotions impact others.

7. Seek Professional Help: If you are struggling to develop your emotional intelligence, seek professional help from a therapist or counselor. They can provide the necessary tools and support to build your emotional intelligence.

Emotional intelligence is crucial in building healthy relationships. It involves being aware of one's emotions, understanding them, and effectively managing them. Here are some ways to develop emotional intelligence:

1. Recognize and acknowledge emotions: To develop emotional intelligence, it is essential first to recognize and accept one's emotions. This means identifying and labeling the emotions one is feeling rather than denying or ignoring them.

2. Develop empathy: Empathy is the ability to understand and share another person's feelings. Developing empathy involves actively listening

to others, being non-judgmental, and putting oneself in the other person's shoes.

3. Practice self-awareness: Self-awareness involves understanding one's emotions and how they impact thoughts, behavior, and relationships. To develop self-awareness, engaging in self-reflection, journaling, or seeking feedback from others is essential.

4. Manage emotions effectively: Emotional intelligence also involves managing emotions effectively. This means being able to regulate one's emotions and respond appropriately to the feelings of others.

5. Build healthy relationships: Developing emotional intelligence is essential in building healthy relationships. It involves being respectful, open, and honest with others and being able to communicate effectively.

6. Seek professional help: If emotional intelligence is a struggle, seeking professional help from a therapist or counselor can be beneficial in developing emotional intelligence and improving relationships.

Emotional intelligence is a vital component of healthy relationships. Developing emotional intelligence involves:

- Recognizing and acknowledging emotions.
- Developing empathy.
- Practicing self-awareness.
- Managing emotions effectively.
- Building healthy relationships.

- Seeking professional help if necessary.

By developing emotional intelligence, individuals can improve their relationships and overall well-being.

Chapter 3

Nurturing Positive Relationships

To build and maintain positive relationships, it is essential to prioritize mutual respect, effective communication, and empathy. Here are some critical strategies for nurturing positive relationships:

1. Active Listening: Effective communication is critical to building positive relationships. Active listening involves paying full attention to the person speaking, avoiding interrupting, and clarifying misunderstandings. Listening actively shows that you value and respect the other person's perspective.

2. Empathy: Empathy involves the ability to understand and share the feelings of others. It is essential to recognize and acknowledge the

emotions of others, as well as express empathy and offer support when needed.

3. Respect: Respect is fundamental to any positive relationship. It involves recognizing and valuing the opinions, beliefs, and feelings of others. Respectful behavior also involves setting boundaries, avoiding derogatory or dismissive language, and treating others with kindness and compassion.

4. Honesty: Honesty is a critical component of positive relationships. Being truthful and transparent fosters trust and mutual respect. Being honest also involves owning up to mistakes and taking responsibility for your actions.

5. Positivity: Positivity involves maintaining a positive outlook and focusing on the good in others. It consists in avoiding criticism, judgment, and negativity. It also involves expressing appreciation and gratitude towards others for their contributions and support.

6. Flexibility: Flexibility involves being open to change and adapting to new situations. It consists in being willing to compromise and find common ground. Flexibility also involves recognizing and respecting the unique perspectives and needs of others.

7. Forgiveness involves letting go of past hurts and resentments and choosing to move forward with a positive outlook. Forgiveness is essential to building and maintaining positive relationships, as it allows for the opportunity to repair and

strengthen relationships that may have been damaged.

You can nurture positive relationships with those around you by prioritizing active listening, empathy, respect, honesty, positivity, flexibility, and forgiveness. These strategies can help you build strong, supportive, and fulfilling connections with family, friends, colleagues, and romantic partners. Remember that positive relationships require effort and commitment, but the rewards are worth it.

Nurturing positive relationships can also involve finding common ground and sharing interests. Engaging in activities you enjoy can deepen your connection and foster a stronger sense of mutual respect and understanding. This can include anything from hobbies and sports to volunteer work and community events.

Another important aspect of nurturing positive relationships is practicing effective communication. This means actively listening to the other person's perspective, expressing your thoughts and feelings clearly and respectfully, and finding ways to work together to overcome challenges or conflicts. It's also important to avoid blame or defensiveness and instead focus on finding solutions that work for both parties.

Finally, nurturing positive relationships requires ongoing effort and attention. It's essential to make time for the people you care about, whether by scheduling regular check-ins or finding ways to stay connected even when you're apart. This can involve everything from sending thoughtful texts or emails to planning a special outing or event together.

Overall, nurturing positive relationships involves being proactive, intentional, and committed to building meaningful connections with the people in your life.

Whether you're focused on strengthening or cultivating new relationships, the key is to approach each interaction with an open heart and a willingness to learn and grow together.

Chapter 4

Understanding the Role of Attachment Styles

Attachment styles refer to the patterns of behaviors, thoughts, and emotions that individuals develop in response to the availability and responsiveness of their caregivers during early childhood. These attachment patterns can significantly impact an individual's ability to form and maintain healthy relationships throughout their life.

There are four main attachment styles: secure attachment, anxious-preoccupied attachment, dismissive-avoidant attachment, and fearful-avoidant attachment.

Secure attachment is characterized by a positive view of self and others, a belief that relationships are generally safe and rewarding, and the ability to seek support when needed. On the other hand, anxious-preoccupied attachment is characterized by a negative view of self and a positive view of others, a belief that relationships are uncertain and unstable, and a tendency to seek excessive reassurance from others. Dismissive-avoidant attachment is characterized by a positive view of self and a negative view of others, a belief that relationships are not worth the effort, and a tendency to withdraw emotionally. Finally, fearful-avoidant attachment is characterized by a negative view of self and others, a belief that relationships are painful and confusing, and a tendency to desire and fear intimacy.

It is important to note that attachment styles are not fixed or immutable. They can change over time as individuals gain new experiences and insights about themselves and their relationships. However, identifying one's attachment style can be a useful starting point for understanding relationship behavior patterns and working towards greater emotional regulation and connection.

Nurturing positive relationships can involve developing skills such as effective communication, active listening, empathy, and conflict resolution. These skills can be learned through therapy, self-reflection, and practice in everyday interactions with others. It is also important to cultivate self-awareness and self-care, as individuals with solid self-worth and self-esteem are better equipped to form and maintain healthy relationships.

Understanding and addressing attachment styles can also be vital in nurturing positive relationships. For individuals with insecure attachment styles, therapy can be a helpful resource for working through past traumas and developing new coping mechanisms. It can also involve working towards greater emotional regulation and self-awareness and practicing new patterns of behavior in relationships.

Ultimately, nurturing positive relationships involves ongoing effort and commitment. It requires a willingness to reflect on one's behavior patterns and make changes as needed, as well as a commitment to open communication and a desire to work through challenges and conflicts healthily and constructively. With time and effort, individuals can develop the skills and mindset necessary to form and maintain fulfilling relationships with others.

Individuals who have experienced inconsistent or neglectful caregiving during childhood will likely develop an anxious attachment style. They crave constant reassurance and have a fear of abandonment. As a result, these individuals can become clingy and possessive, often pushing their partner away, thus reinforcing their fear of abandonment.

On the other hand, individuals who have experienced parental overprotection or criticism may develop an avoidant attachment style. They often fear intimacy and become emotionally distant from their partners. These individuals can dismiss their partner's needs and often struggle to communicate effectively.

On the other hand, secure attachment styles are developed when an individual has experienced consistent, responsive caregiving during childhood. They feel comfortable with emotional intimacy and can communicate effectively with their partners. They can give and receive love and support in healthy ways.

Recognizing attachment styles can be crucial in developing positive and healthy relationships. In addition, understanding the roots of one's attachment style can also help individuals work towards overcoming negative patterns and behaviors in relationships.

It is also important to note that attachment styles can change over time and with therapy. However, with self-awareness and intentional efforts, individuals can work towards developing a more secure attachment style and building healthy relationships.

Chapter 5

Coping with Envy and Jealousy

Envy and jealousy are two of the most uncomfortable emotions one can experience. These emotions can arise when we feel threatened or compare ourselves to others. Of course, it is normal to feel these emotions occasionally, but it is essential to know how to manage them so they do not consume us. Here are some ways to cope with envy and jealousy:

1. Acknowledge and accept your feelings: The first step in coping with envy and jealousy is acknowledging and getting that you are feeling these emotions. It is important not to suppress or deny these feelings as they will only grow stronger.

2. Identify the source of your envy or jealousy: Once you have accepted your feelings, try to

identify the source of your envy or jealousy. Is a particular person, situation, or achievement triggering these emotions? Understanding your feelings' basis can help you address the root cause.

3. Practice gratitude: Envy and jealousy can make it difficult to appreciate what we have. Practicing gratitude can shift our focus from what we lack to what we have. Take time each day to reflect on what you are grateful for.

4. Focus on your strengths: Comparing ourselves to others can be slippery. Instead of focusing on what others have that we do not, focusing on our strengths and accomplishments is essential. This can help boost our self-esteem and reduce envy and jealousy.

5. Set realistic goals: Envy and jealousy can arise when others achieve more than us. Setting realistic goals for ourselves and focusing on our progress rather than comparing ourselves to others is essential.

6. Practice self-care: Envy and jealousy can be emotionally draining. It is essential to take care of ourselves both physically and mentally. This can include getting enough sleep, eating well, exercising, and practicing mindfulness or meditation.

7. Seek support: If feelings of envy or jealousy are causing significant distress, seeking permission from a therapist or counselor may be helpful. They can help you identify your feelings'

underlying causes and develop strategies to manage them effectively.

One effective way to deal with jealousy is to challenge the negative thoughts that often accompany it. Instead of allowing ourselves to spiral into a cycle of negative self-talk, we can practice acknowledging our feelings while challenging the distorted beliefs that fuel them. For example, it can be helpful to ask ourselves questions like, "Is this thought based on facts or assumptions?" or "How likely is this worst-case scenario I'm imagining?" Examining our thoughts more objectively allows us to gain perspective and see things more clearly.

Another strategy for coping with jealousy is to practice self-compassion. Instead of berating ourselves for feeling jealous or inadequate, we can practice extending the same kindness and understanding to ourselves that we would go to a good friend. This can involve acknowledging our feelings without judgment, reminding ourselves that it's okay to feel vulnerable sometimes, and seeking out activities that make us feel good about ourselves.

Additionally, practicing gratitude can be a powerful tool for managing jealousy. By focusing on the good things in our lives, we can shift our attention away from what we don't have and toward what we do. This can help us cultivate a sense of abundance and contentment rather than feeling like we're constantly in a state of lack or comparison.

Finally, it's important to remember that jealousy is a natural and normal human emotion. We all feel it sometimes, and it doesn't mean we're flawed or unlovable. However, by acknowledging our jealousy, practicing self-compassion, challenging our negative thoughts, and cultivating gratitude, we can learn to manage these difficult emotions in healthy and productive ways.

Chapter 6

Building a Supportive Environment for Change

Change is difficult, especially when addressing complex issues like abuse or harmful behaviors. It can be overwhelming and lonely to tackle these problems on your own. However, building a supportive environment can make all the difference in the journey toward healing and growth. This chapter will explore ways to create a supportive network and domain for change.

1. Identify your support system: The first step in building a supportive environment is identifying the people who can help you on this journey. This may include friends, family members, therapists, support groups, or other professionals who specialize in the area you are trying to address. It's important to remember that not everyone in your life can provide the support you need, so it's okay to reach out to others who can.

2. Communicate your needs: Once you have
    identified your support system, you must
    communicate your needs to them. Let them
    know what you are struggling with, what you
    need from them, and how they can best support
    you. This will help them understand what you're
    going through and how they can help you.

3. Set boundaries: Building a supportive
    environment also means setting boundaries with
    those around you. This may mean limiting
    contact with people who trigger negative
    emotions or behaviors or setting boundaries with
    loved ones who may unintentionally enable
    unhealthy patterns. Boundaries are essential in
    creating a safe and supportive environment for
    change.

4. Focus on positive relationships: Surrounding
    yourself with positive relationships can be a
    powerful motivator for change. Seek out people
    who inspire and support you, who encourage you
    to be your best self. Positive relationships can
    help boost your self-esteem and provide a sense
    of belonging and support.

5. Practice self-care: Taking care of yourself is
    essential in building a supportive environment
    for change. Make sure to prioritize self-care
    activities like exercise, meditation, or hobbies
    that bring you joy. When you care for yourself,
    you'll be better equipped to handle the challenges
    of change.

6. Seek professional help: Professional help can be
    a valuable resource in building a supportive

environment for change. Therapists or other professionals can help you identify and address underlying issues contributing to negative behaviors. They can also provide guidance and support as you work towards your goals.

Building a supportive environment for change can be challenging, but it is essential for those seeking personal growth and transformation. Here are some additional tips for creating a supportive environment:

1. Surround yourself with positive people: The people around you can significantly impact your life. Surround yourself with people who support your goals, encourage your growth, and inspire you to be your best self.

2. Set healthy boundaries: Healthy boundaries are essential for protecting your mental and emotional well-being. Set boundaries with people who are negative, toxic, or unsupportive of your growth.

3. Practice self-care: Self-care is crucial for maintaining your physical, emotional, and mental health. Take time to care for yourself, whether exercising, meditating, getting enough sleep, or engaging in hobbies you enjoy.

4. Seek professional support: You may need professional help to create a supportive environment. Seek a therapist, counselor, or coach who can help you navigate challenges and provide guidance on creating a more supportive environment.

5. Focus on progress, not perfection: It's important
    to remember that creating a supportive
    environment is a process that won't happen
    overnight. Celebrate your progress, no matter
    how small, and be patient with yourself as you
    work towards your goals.

By implementing these strategies, you can create a
supportive environment that will help you achieve your
personal growth goals and overcome any obstacles that
come your way. Remember, change is possible, and you
have the power to create the life you want.

Chapter 7

Cultivating Gratitude and Positivity

Life can be challenging, and getting caught up in negative thoughts and emotions is easy. However, focusing on the positive aspects of life can help you feel more content, satisfied, and fulfilled. Cultivating gratitude and positivity is an essential aspect of emotional and mental wellbeing. In this chapter, we will explore strategies to help you develop a positive mindset and an attitude of gratitude.

1. Practice Mindfulness

Mindfulness is being present and fully engaged at the moment without judgment. Mindfulness can help you cultivate a positive mindset by enabling you to focus on the present moment and appreciate what you have. In addition, mindfulness practices such as meditation, breathing exercises, and yoga can help you reduce stress and anxiety, improve your mood, and increase your overall wellbeing.

2.   Keep a Gratitude Journal

Keeping a gratitude journal can be an effective way to cultivate a positive attitude. Each day, write down a few things that you are grateful for. These can be big or small, from a sunny day to a good cup of coffee to a supportive friend or family member. Reflecting on the positive aspects of your life can help shift your mindset towards positivity and gratitude.

3.   Focus on Solutions

When faced with a challenge or obstacle, it's easy to get bogged down in negative thoughts and emotions. However, focusing on solutions rather than dwelling on problems can help you cultivate a positive mindset. Instead of getting frustrated or upset, take a step back and assess the situation. Then, brainstorm potential solutions and take action to address the issue.

4.   Surround Yourself with Positive People

The people you surround yourself with can significantly impact your mindset and emotions. Surrounding yourself with positive, supportive people can help you cultivate a positive attitude and a sense of gratitude. Seek out people who lift you, inspire you, and make you feel good about yourself.

5.   Practice Self-Care

Taking care of yourself is an essential aspect of cultivating a positive mindset. Self-care can help you reduce stress, increase your sense of wellbeing, and develop a positive attitude. Self-care practices can include getting enough sleep, eating healthy, exercising regularly, and engaging in activities that bring you joy and fulfillment.

6.   Focus on the Good

Getting caught up in negative news and media is easy, but focusing on the good can help you cultivate a positive mindset. Instead of watching or reading negative information, seek positive stories and media that inspire and uplift you. Focus on the good in the world, and you will start seeing more positivity in your life.

7.   Practice Random Acts of Kindness

Practicing random acts of kindness can help you cultivate a positive mindset and an attitude of gratitude. Small acts of kindness, such as buying someone a coffee or sending a thoughtful text message, can make a big difference in someone's day. Practicing compassion can also help you feel more connected to others and increase your overall wellbeing.

Cultivating gratitude and positivity can be a challenging but rewarding process. It involves making a conscious effort to shift your focus away from negative thoughts and emotions and, instead, embracing the positive aspects of your life. Here are some tips to help you cultivate gratitude and positivity in your life:

1.   Start a gratitude journal: Take a few minutes daily to write down things you are grateful for. This can be as simple as a good cup of coffee in the morning or as significant as a supportive friend or family member.

2.   Practice mindfulness: Mindfulness meditation can help you become more aware of your

thoughts and emotions. It can also help you focus on the present moment and release negative thoughts.

3. Surround yourself with positive people: Spend time with people who uplift and inspire you. Negative people can bring you down and make it challenging to stay positive.

4. Engage in activities that bring you joy: Whether taking a walk in nature, cooking a favorite meal, or spending time with loved ones, make time for activities that bring you joy.

5. Practice self-care: Take care of yourself physically, emotionally, and mentally. This includes getting enough sleep, eating a healthy diet, and exercising regularly.

6. Use positive affirmations: Repeat positive affirmations to yourself daily, such as "I am capable," "I am worthy," and "I am enough."

7. Express gratitude to others: Show gratitude to those around you by showing appreciation for their kindness and support.

8. Focus on the good: When faced with a challenging situation, try to focus on the positive aspects rather than dwelling on the negative.

9. Give back to others: Volunteer your time or donate to a cause that you are passionate about. Giving back to others can bring a sense of fulfillment and gratitude.

10. Celebrate small victories: Take time to celebrate small achievements and progress towards your

goals. This can help you stay motivated and positive.

By incorporating these practices into your daily life, you can cultivate gratitude and positivity, leading to greater happiness and fulfillment. Remember that developing these habits takes time and effort, but the rewards are well worth it.

Chapter 8

Seeking Professional Help for Detoxifying Personality

Detoxifying your personality can be an intensive and challenging journey. It involves working through deep-seated patterns of behavior that may have been established over a long period. While some individuals can successfully navigate this journey on their own, others may require professional help to overcome the obstacles in their path. Seeking professional help can be a crucial step in the detoxification process and provide individuals with the tools and support they need to make meaningful changes.

If you are considering seeking professional help for detoxifying your personality, several options are available. The most common forms of professional service include therapy, counseling, and coaching. Each approach offers unique benefits, and the right direction for you depends on your needs and preferences.

Therapy is a type of professional help often recommended for individuals struggling with deep-seated patterns of behavior or thought. Therapists are trained to help individuals explore their emotions and thought patterns and to develop new coping mechanisms and strategies for managing challenging situations. Common types of therapy include cognitive-behavioral, psychodynamic, and dialectical behavior therapy. Counseling is another form of professional help that can be helpful for individuals who are struggling with issues related to their personality or behavior. Counselors are trained to guide and support individuals facing challenging situations or transitions and can help individuals develop new coping strategies and communication skills. Some common types of counseling include individual, group, and family counseling.

Coaching is a third option for individuals who are looking for professional help in detoxifying their personalities. Coaches are trained to help individuals set and achieve goals and can provide support and guidance throughout the process. While coaching may not be appropriate for individuals dealing with more serious mental health issues, it can be a powerful tool for individuals looking to make meaningful changes in their lives.

Regardless of which type of professional help you choose, it is essential to find an experienced and qualified provider to help you. Look for providers who are licensed and trained in their field and who have a track record of success in working with individuals who are struggling with similar issues. You may also seek out providers who specialize in the specific type of help you seek, whether therapy, counseling, or coaching.

In addition to seeking professional help, there are several things you can do on your own to support your detoxification journey. These may include practicing self-care, setting boundaries with toxic people, and engaging in activities that bring you joy and fulfillment. It is also essential to be patient and compassionate as you navigate this process and remember that change takes time and effort.

Detoxifying your personality can be challenging, but with the right tools and support, it is possible to make meaningful and lasting changes in your life. If you are considering seeking professional help for this process, take the time to research your options and find a provider who can help you achieve your goals. And remember, no matter how difficult the journey may be, the rewards of a healthier, happier, and more authentic life are well worth the effort.

Various professionals and resources are available to support individuals seeking to detoxify their personalities. Some of these include:

1. Therapists: A therapist or counselor can provide a safe and confidential space for individuals to explore their thoughts, feelings, and behaviors. They can also teach individuals coping skills and healthy ways of expressing themselves.

2. Psychologists: Psychologists can help individuals understand the root causes of their problematic behaviors and provide evidence-based strategies for overcoming them.

3. Support groups: Support groups, such as Alcoholics Anonymous or Narcotics

Anonymous, provide a community of individuals who are going through similar struggles. These groups offer a non-judgmental space for sharing experiences and gaining insight.

4. Self-help books and resources: Many self-help books and online resources are available that guide how to detoxify one's personality. These resources may offer mindfulness, cognitive-behavioral therapy, or meditation techniques.

5. Life coaches: Life coaches can guide and support individuals seeking to make positive changes in their lives. They can help individuals set goals, create action plans, and hold them accountable for making progress.

It's important to note that seeking professional help to detoxify one's personality is not a sign of weakness but a courageous step towards self-improvement. Finding a professional or resource that resonates with you and aligns with your goals and values is essential. Additionally, it's essential to maintain a commitment to self-reflection and self-improvement outside of professional help. This can include practicing self-care, maintaining healthy relationships, and staying connected to one's values and goals. By visiting committed to growth and self-improvement, individuals can create a supportive environment for lasting change.

Chapter 9

Encouraging Loved ones to Overcome Toxic Traits

Dealing with a loved one with toxic traits can be emotionally draining and challenging. It can also take a toll on your relationship and affect your well-being. While it's ultimately up to the individual to seek help and work on themselves, there are things you can do to encourage them to take steps toward growth and change.

1. Approach the topic with compassion and empathy - It's essential to approach the subject of toxic behavior with care and kindness. Criticizing or blaming your loved one can create a defensive response, making it harder for them to take constructive criticism. Try to approach the conversation with an understanding of their

struggles and challenges, and offer your support and encouragement.

2. Focus on the behavior, not the person - When discussing toxic behavior, it's essential to focus on the action or behavior rather than the individual. Avoid personal attacks or character judgments, which can be hurtful and counterproductive. Instead, please provide specific examples of behavior you find concerning and how it affects you and your relationship.

3. Express your concerns and feelings - Let your loved one know how their behavior affects you and your relationship. Express your concerns and emotions in a calm and non-confrontational way, and avoid being accusatory. Use "I" statements to communicate how their behavior makes you feel rather than making assumptions about their intentions or motivations.

4. Encourage them to seek professional help - While offering your support and encouragement is crucial, it's also essential to encourage your loved one to seek professional help. A licensed therapist or counselor can provide the tools and support necessary to address and overcome toxic behavior patterns.

5. Set boundaries - If your loved one is unwilling or unable to seek help, it may be necessary to set boundaries in the relationship. This can include establishing clear expectations and consequences for their behavior. Sticking to these boundaries

and holding your loved one accountable for their actions is essential.

6. Practice self-care - Dealing with a loved one's toxic behavior can be emotionally taxing. It's crucial to prioritize self-care and care for your mental and emotional health. This can include setting aside time for self-care activities, practicing mindfulness, and seeking support from friends, family, or a therapist.

Encouraging a loved one to overcome toxic behavior patterns can be a challenging and emotional journey. However, it is possible to encourage growth and positive change with compassion, empathy, and support. Remember to focus on the behavior, express your concerns and feelings, encourage them to seek professional help, set boundaries, and prioritize self-care. It is possible to cultivate a healthy and supportive relationship with time and effort.

Encouraging loved ones to overcome toxic traits can be challenging, but it is necessary for their well-being and the health of your relationship. Here are some ways to support them:

1. Be compassionate: Show empathy and understanding toward their struggles. Let them know that you are there to support them and that you believe in their ability to change.

2. Focus on behavior, not the person: It is essential to separate the person from their behavior. Criticize the behavior, not the individual. This can help your loved one understand that you are not attacking them but rather their toxic trait.

3. Encourage self-reflection: Encourage your loved one to reflect on their actions and their impact on others. This can help them become more aware of their behavior and how it affects those around them.

4. Suggest therapy: Suggest that they seek professional help. A therapist can provide a safe and supportive environment for your loved one to explore their thoughts and feelings and work towards changing their toxic traits.

5. Be patient: Changing toxic behavior is a process that takes time. Be patient with your loved one and continue to offer support throughout their journey.

6. Lead by example: Model positive behavior and traits for your loved one to emulate. This can inspire them to work towards positive change.

7. Set boundaries: It is essential to set boundaries and communicate them clearly with your loved one. This can help them understand what behaviors are not acceptable and what the consequences of those behaviors may be.

In summary, encouraging loved ones to overcome toxic traits requires compassion, patience, and support. By focusing on behavior, encouraging self-reflection, suggesting therapy, leading by example, and setting boundaries, you can help your loved one on their journey towards positive change.

Chapter 10

Embracing a Journey of Continuous Self-Growth

Personal growth and self-improvement are ongoing processes that require a solid commitment to oneself. Embracing this journey requires a deep understanding of one's strengths and weaknesses and a willingness to challenge oneself to become a better person.

To begin the journey of continuous self-improvement, it's essential to establish clear goals and intentions. These goals can be short-term or long-term, and they should align with your values and vision for your life. In addition, developing a growth mindset is essential, which means adopting an openness, curiosity, and willingness to learn.

One of the critical components of self-improvement is self-awareness. This involves taking an honest look at oneself, examining past behaviors and patterns, and identifying areas for improvement. Practicing self-reflection through journaling, meditation, or therapy can help develop this self-awareness.

Another important aspect of self-improvement is developing healthy habits and routines. This includes adopting a nutritious diet, regular exercise, and good sleep hygiene. These habits can support physical and mental health, which is essential for personal growth.

It's also essential to seek out resources and support. This can include attending workshops, reading self-help books, or seeking guidance from a mentor or therapist. Engaging in community activities and building a network of supportive friends and family can also be beneficial.

Finally, it's essential to recognize that the journey of self-improvement can be challenging. There will be setbacks and challenges, but staying committed and maintaining a positive attitude is necessary. Celebrate progress, no matter how small, and use setbacks as opportunities for growth and learning.

In conclusion, embracing a journey of continuous self-improvement requires a commitment to oneself and a willingness to challenge oneself. Developing self-awareness, healthy habits, and seeking resources and support are essential components of this journey. With perseverance and a growth mindset, anyone can achieve personal growth and self-improvement.